WORKOUT TO REACH OUT

WHY FITNESS IS IMPORTANT TO YOUR WALK WITH GOD AND HOW TO ACHIEVE IT!

By Health and Physical Education Teacher,
ACE Certified Personal Trainer, and Military Veteran

Jason Berry

www.workout2reachout.com

CROSSLINK
PUBLISHING

Workout to Reach Out: WHY fitness is important to your walk with God and HOW to achieve it!

CrossLink Publishing
www.crosslinkpublishing.com

ISBN 978-1-63357-043-6

Library of Congress Control Number: 2015946283

All Scripture quotations are taken from the NEW AMERICAN STANDARD BIBLE®, Copyright © 1960, 1962, 1963, 1968, 1971, 1972, 1973, 1975, 1977, 1995 by The Lockman Foundation. Used by permission.

WORKOUT TO REACH OUT

Contents

Jason Berry joined the Pennsylvania Army National Guard in 2009 as an infantry soldier. Upon completing Airborne School, Jason joined his unit in Iraq in support of Operation Iraqi Freedom. Jason served a total of seven years in the military and was a team leader. He had the privilege of witnessing to many of his teammates and watched God move mightily within his unit.

In 2013 Jason graduated from Messiah College with a bachelor's degree in health and physical education. This will be Jason's third year of teaching at a local high school. Jason is an ACE certified personal trainer and enjoys helping people take care of their bodies so that they can maximize the call of God on their life.

Jason is a proud member of Church Without Walls in Harrisburg, Pennsylvania, where he serves in young adult and youth ministry. He is extremely happy and blessed to be married to his amazing wife, Sandy. Together they are both very passionate about spreading God's Word and advancing His kingdom.

CONTACT JASON

For personal training, speaking events, testimonies, or faith and fitness seminars, contact Jason at www.workout2reachout.com

Acknowledgements

T hank you Lord, for helping me to write this book! I pray that the book brings You glory and honor and helps people walk closer with You. Thank you to everyone who helped to make this book possible, including but not limited to:

My wife, Sandy, for outstanding pictures, editing, encouragement, love, and discernment. Pastors Philip and Gwen Thornton for helping me to walk closer with God, build my faith, and edit the book. All of my family for constant love, advice, and support. Todd G Photography for fantastic pictures. STHS for allowing me to utilize their facility for pictures. Cheryl and Becky for editing my book and providing such positive feedback. The "daughters of thunder" (April, Perdeta, Cheryl, Matea, and Jess) for great workouts. All of the members of FAYTH (Fellowship Among Young-adults To Hear the Word). Team SnH (Strength and Honor). All of my church family and friends. Thank you and I hope you enjoy the book!

A Transformation Unfolds ... and the Journey Goes

From early teens to maybe age thirty, I was characterized as energetic, physically active, and focused. After a series of unforeseen events, my body suffered severe injuries from unexplained accidents and began to yield to symptomatic and chronic pain, thus leading to severe obesity, disease, and depression from the vicious cycles. At the close of 2014, it appeared that only a miraculous healing could change the outcome of my future.

Wouldn't you know I just happened to be at our traditional Christmas family gathering to watch Jason Berry open his brand new set of digital dumbbells. Within minutes of unwrapping the equipment, he began to share how excited he was about finishing his book, and mentioned that if I desired to start a workout program, he would make himself available.

My first horrific thoughts were, *Oh no, are you kidding? Do you realize how fragile my framework is? Did you forget I was the one at your summer boot camp who couldn't hold a water jug, who couldn't stand up for the five-minute warmup, who bailed out and never finished, completed, or got through one session? That body!* Then came the thought, *My joints are so impaired. After eight weeks of physical therapy in November, there was no improvement.*

But then my mind flipped over to what-ifs. What if he can really help me? What if I can feel better? What if these bones can live again? It wasn't the fact that he offered; it was the way he said it and the faith guarantee behind it. I consented and decided to let him train me. Praise God for that decision!

As of this writing, it has been seven miraculous, overcoming months since the start of a new mind-set and workout sessions with Jason. My energy level has tripled. My cellular, molecular, structural, and cardio levels have improved. Pounds have flown off. Measurements have shrunk. And I AM THE HEALED OF THE LORD! Every week I thank God for new victories, new goals, new accomplishments, and less of me when I see my reflection.

You may be wondering or thinking, *There was no mentioning about the exact number of pounds, inches, nor dress sizes lost.* The reason is because at the end of the day, when the music stops, what is most important to me is that this transformation has divine supernatural purpose in the earth.

Thank you, Jason, for filling a void in the body of Christ. I think everyone needs to have a copy of this book. It is a powerful and anointed teaching tool. As a reader, you're in for a real treat. Get ready to go on a journey, just like I did.

F acts are subject to change. Truth is eternal. I want you to shake off any doubts, fears, or past experiences that cut down negatively on you as a person. Your past has no future. It doesn't matter what the past says about you. It matters what God says about you ... and He has called you for greatness.

God has called you to do mighty things for Him, but are you prepared to maximize that calling? Your body is the vessel by which you preach the gospel and live out your life. This vessel needs to be healthy! Working out enables you to reach out. It enables you to maintain a state of physical fitness and health that is prepared to meet every challenge. Full of energy, joy, and purpose, your walk with God will skyrocket to a new level.

There are many different reasons why you may have picked up this book. Maybe you want to know how fitness relates to your life as a Christian. Or maybe you want to know what God's Word says about getting in shape instead of what society tells you. Perhaps you aren't a Christian at all and are curious to this book's viewpoint on fitness. Are you the person that has been stuck in a cycle of obesity and has tried many ways to break the cycle but nothing has worked?

Regardless of why you picked up this book, prepare to learn why taking care of your body is important to God and how to accomplish that! If you have been stuck in obesity, worry, obsessing about your body image, or feeling inadequate, get ready to be set free! Jesus has already done everything He needed for you to have victory in EVERY area of your life.

Chapter 1

WHO YOU ARE

Let me start off by saying that you are not defined by your body image! Whatever condition you are in right now physically, that does not define who you are. What defines you as a person is the Spirit of God in you. God loves you and has wonderful plans for your life!

Don't look down on yourself as a person if you are currently overweight, not in shape, or unhealthy. However, being unhealthy is not God's best for you, and He has given you power through the blood of Jesus to change this status! To understand why you should change it, and why it's important to be fit, allow me to first establish the foundation of who you really are.

When God created the heavens and the earth, He spoke to those things. But when God created mankind, and you, He spoke to **Himself**, saying, "Let **Us** make man in **Our** image, according to **Our** likeness," in Genesis 1:26. We see this again in verse 27, "God created man in **His own image**, in the image of God He created him; male and female He created them." You are created in the image and likeness of God! You are God's best idea and His most treasured creation.

In the Garden of Eden, mankind was like God and was righteous, had authority, had dominion, was in perfect health, had no poverty, no disease, and no sickness. When Adam and Eve sinned, they lost the likeness of God. They were no longer righteous, but were tainted with sin. Adam and Eve were now subject to the consequences of sin. The "wages of sin is death" (Romans 6:23). This death included spiritual death (being separated from God) and eventually physical death. Sin also brought fear, guilt, pain, and sickness into the world.

Just like Adam and Eve, we have sinned and rebelled against God's commandments. Romans 3:23 tells us that "all have sinned and fallen short of the glory of God." No matter how many good deeds you do, you are still a sinner, have lost the likeness of God, have lost righteousness, and deserve to go to Hell! Your works can't save you, and you can't earn back righteousness. We need a savior! We need a hero!

Praise God that He did not leave His chosen creation in this state! God had a redemptive plan from the beginning to bring you back to Himself. You are created to be in relationship with God as His son or daughter! "For God so loved the world, that He gave His only begotten Son, that whoever believes in Him shall not perish but have eternal life" (John 3:16).

God sent His son, Jesus Christ, into the world. Jesus came in the flesh, fully God but also fully human, and was tempted with everything we are tempted with but without sin. Jesus took all of our sin upon Him and took the penalty of sin for us. He died on the cross so that your relationship with God might be restored. He died so you might have eternal life with Him instead of being in hell. He has removed your sin as far as the east is from the west.

Believers in Jesus have their dirty garments cast off and are now clothed with the garments of salvation! You have the gift of eternal life and have been made righteous if you accept what Jesus did for you. It is by faith in Christ that you are saved and receive everything that Jesus has restored. You must believe in what He did for you and ask Him to come into your heart. With your mouth, you confess Him as Lord and Savior and begin the process of living for the One who died and rose again on your behalf!

But Jesus didn't ONLY come so that you would go to heaven. His sacrifice on the cross for you is not just fire insurance! Jesus said that He came "that they might have life and life abundantly" (John 10:10). Jesus has restored the likeness of God back unto you and wants you to walk as His son or daughter on the earth! Second Corinthians 5:21 states that, "He made Him who knew no sin to be sin on our behalf, so that we might become the righteousness of God in Him."

In Christ, you are now made righteous. When God looks at you, He doesn't see your sin, doesn't see your past or your mistakes, and definitely isn't looking at your body composition! If you're in Christ, then God sees a righteous restored child of God that is called to do the works that Jesus did!

The life that you now live does not have to include sickness, disease, poverty, or defeat! Jesus didn't die for you so you could suffer on this earth as a defeated Christian and hide in a corner until you go to heaven. God has awesome plans for His children and has anointed them to advance His kingdom, overcome darkness, cast out demons, lay hands on the sick, do good, spread the gospel, and set the oppressed free! See Mark chapter 16. He has empowered believers in His name by the Holy Spirit to do the works that He did and other greater works!

Jesus stated, "Truly, truly, I say to you, he who believes in Me, the works that I do, he will do also; and greater works than these he will do; because I go to the Father" (John 14:12). While all of these blessings are available to believers, the key to accessing them is by using your faith on purpose.

WAKE UP CALL!

I accepted Jesus Christ into my heart at a very young age. Praise God for parents that believed! But I really didn't understand the fullness of my identity in Christ until I was twenty years old. Up until this point, I had put limits on what God could do through me. I was waiting to hear his voice tell me what to do. I didn't realize that His Word had already called me into action. I didn't understand that I was already qualified for greatness by what Jesus had done for me. God knew my hunger for Him, and my world was about to get turned upside down…literally.

The rain pelted the windshield as I curled around the winding road in my Jeep Wrangler. The rain clouds had swept in rapidly, darkening the brightness of the new morning. Back from my deployment to Iraq, I was working on earning my health and physical education degree at Messiah College. It was an easy half-hour commute from my parents' house to get there. But this day was different.

As I came around a sharp turn at the crest of a hill, my Jeep skidded into the left lane. I wasn't speeding, but the slippery roads had caught me off guard. As my Jeep entered the left lane, I noticed that another car was barreling down the road at me head-on! I yanked the steering wheel hard to the right to avoid the car and lined myself up to hit the hill alongside the road. I slammed the brakes in an attempt to avoid the hill, which threw my jeep into a spin. Before I knew it, my jeep hit the side of the hill and rolled uncontrollably along the road.

My Jeep ended up on its side with the driver side door facing the ground. Military instinct kicked in and I knew that I had to get out of the car right away. My Jeep was dangerously sitting in the middle of the right lane. You couldn't see me from the other side of the hill that I had just crested. Any car coming over that hill would only have seconds to dodge before ramming me. And there would be no stop to more cars coming over the hill, no warning. This situation had the potential to be a multicar accident where many people could have been hurt or lost their lives. But God was with me.

I kicked out the passenger side door above me and climbed out of the Jeep within twenty seconds after the accident. To my amazement, there was already a man at the top of the hill siphoning traffic around me. I ran down the opposing way to stop traffic as I called 911. Within minutes, police, a tow truck, my parents, and my brother had all arrived. No one was hurt. Upon examining myself, I realized that I didn't even have a scratch! The only damage done was to my Jeep, which was back in action within a couple of weeks.

I never got to thank the man at the top of the hill. He simply disappeared. Whether it was an angel or a servant of God that He had put in the right place, I don't know. Either way, I knew it was a miracle for him to be siphoning traffic twenty seconds after the accident. And for me to not have a single scratch! I heard the voice of God clearer that day than I ever had before. It wasn't a booming voice out of heaven, but a still small voice that I could hear in my spirit. God spoke to me, "Jason, you have known me your whole life, but there is something more."

What did God mean by saying "there was something more"? What had I been missing? I didn't have to wait for the answer long. Two days later, I started dating my amazing wife, Sandy. She brought me to her church that Sunday, and I found the "more" that God was talking about. Church Without Walls in Harrisburg, Pennsylvania, was unlike any church I had ever encountered. In the military and on my own, I had visited dozens of different churches. But I had never experienced a church like this!

The love was real, the fellowship was real, and the power of God was real! Miracles weren't a thing of the past; they occurred in this church every day! I watched countless people be healed, delivered, and set free. Instead of a dry message, God's Word was living and active. I felt the presence of God like never before, and I began to praise Him with all my might! There was "more" to life than what I had thought. I realized that I didn't have to wait for God to call me, but that He already had!

There are many blessings and freedoms that we have through faith in Christ. Allow me to briefly point some of them out to you. Perhaps they will be a "wake-up call" to you like they were to me. By understanding who you are and the calling on your life, you will then understand why fitness is SO important. The fitness part of the book is up next, but you will be glad that you understand the foundation and groundwork!

BLESSINGS, FREEDOMS, AND RESTORED LIKENESS THAT WE HAVE THROUGH FAITH IN CHRIST

Cleansed from Sin/Made Righteous

Jesus has taken away the sin of the world. Before Jesus, the Israelites (a people whom God had chosen to show Himself strong through) would sacrifice animals that would "cover" their sin. However, the Israelites had to offer up sacrifices continually to cover the people. This was an ongoing process, and Hebrews 10:4 states that "it is impossible for the blood of bulls and goats to take away sins." These sacrifices covered the Israelite's sin for a short time, but their sin was never taken away. They would have to offer up these sacrifices year after year.

When John the Baptist saw Jesus, he said, "Behold the lamb of God who **takes away** the sin of the world!" (John 1:21). Jesus has removed sin from all of those that believe in Him by faith. Your sin is taken away and completely forgiven!

Children of God

First John 3:1 states, "See how great a love the Father has bestowed on us, that we would be called children of God; and such we are." Jesus has restored back our relationship with the Father as children of God. The Bible says, "For all who are being led by the Spirit of God, these are the sons of God" (Romans 8:14). When you are led by the Spirit of God, then you are a son or daughter of God!

God is not far off; He is near to those who seek Him. He wants to have a relationship with you and loves you so much that He gave His only begotten Son for you! God wants good things for His children. Not only has He prepared Heaven for you, but He also wants you to walk as a victorious child of God in the earth right now! He wants His sons and daughters to continue His work.

Doing the Work of the Father

A son or daughter learns from their parents and becomes like them. Just as Jesus did the work of His Father, we should be doing the work of our Father! Jesus told his disciples that "as the Father has sent Me, I also send you" (John 20:21). The disciples were people that believed in Jesus and followed Him. Guess what you are? You are called and sent as a disciple, too!

Disciples are more than "fans." A fan sits in the stands and cheers for their team. Jesus hasn't called you to sit in the stands, but to come out on the field and be a game changer. True disciples are committed to imitate their teacher and act like them. Ephesians 5:1 tells us to be "imitators of Christ."

Notice that the disciples were commanded by Jesus to be "teaching them to observe ALL that I commanded you" (Matthew 28:20). These disciples were teaching others to do the work of the Father just like they had learned to do so from Jesus. Miracles, healings, casting out demons, and advancing the kingdom of God are not areas limited to the twelve apostles! That's why Jesus said, "[H]e who BELIEVES in me, the works that I do, he will do also; and greater works than these he will do; because I go to the Father" (John 14:12, with emphasis added).

If we examine God's Word, we'll see many people besides the twelve apostles doing the works of Christ. In Luke 10, we'll see seventy others sent out to preach, heal the sick, and cast out demons in Jesus' name! In Acts, we'll see others once again who are filled with the Holy Spirit and move in power to heal those oppressed by the devil.

In the great commission in Mark 16, Jesus told us, "These signs will accompany those who have believed: in my Name they will cast out demons, they will speak with new tongues; they will pick up serpents, and if they drink any deadly poison, it will not hurt them; they will lay hands on the sick, and they will recover."

No one can do anything apart from Christ. But when you believe in Him, stand in faith in His promises, and are led by His Spirit, then all things are possible! When you preach about God, you don't have to come in words only, but in power and demonstration of the Holy Spirit. You can be filled with the Holy Spirit just as the apostles were and do great works for God!

Ambassadors of Christ

Romans 5:20 tells us that "we are ambassadors for Christ, as though God were making an appeal through us." God wants to work through us to reach the lost and to love people. In our world today, an ambassador is someone who represents his or her country and carries authority from that county. You represent the kingdom of God and come with authority from Heaven.

You don't have to wait to be called by God! He has already called you! God isn't looking for ability, but availability. If you raise your hand and say, "God use me," then He will be the One who will strengthen you and bring out your gifts. Throughout the Bible, God used people who did not feel worthy or up to the task. God didn't give you a spirit of fear but of "power, love, and self-discipline"!

The Enemy is Under Our Feet

First John 3:8 tells us that "the Son of God came to destroy the works of the devil." After Jesus rose again from the dead, He ascended up to Heaven and cleansed the Heavens with His blood (see Hebrews chapters 8, 9, 10). The devil has been cast out of heaven and has "fallen like lightning" (see Revelation 12 and Luke 10).

Satan can never again go up to Heaven to accuse you. The devil is the accuser of the brethren and would do this "day and night" after the "Fall of Man" until the victory of Jesus. We see Satan having access to Heaven before the victory on the cross in books such as Job or Zechariah where he would accuse people in front of God.

But because of Jesus, the accuser of the brethren has been cast down, and he has no place in heaven. He can only accuse you to yourself and try to get you to believe his lies. Jesus said, "Behold, I have given you authority to tread on serpents and scorpions, and **over all the power of the enemy,** and nothing will injure you" (Luke 10:19). Jesus has given us all power and authority over the enemy.

The book of James tells us that when you resist the devil, he will flee from you. Satan can't accuse you before God because the blood of Jesus has made you righteous. The enemy is under your feet. You have power in Jesus' name to cast him out and to trample him. Satan's fate has already been decided, and he will be cast into the fiery hell, along with those who follow him.

Covenant and Blessings

God is a covenant-keeping God. A covenant is an agreement between two parties that can never be broken. It is much stronger than any contract or statement. God's covenants with us are eternal in nature. We have full assurance in them and can stand on them. In Christ, we are under a new covenant based on better promises (see Hebrews).

Even under the old covenant, you'll find that the Israelites were supernaturally blessed when they followed God's commandments. If they were obedient, then the blessings found in Deuteronomy 28 would follow. They were blessed in the city, blessed in the field, blessed in their coming, blessed in their going, and everything they set their hands on prospered. Sickness and disease were removed from their midst. Under Christ, we are under an even better covenant! Jesus took not only your sin upon Himself but a lot of other things, too!

The book of Matthew in chapter 8 tells us that Jesus was fulfilling what was spoken of through Isaiah the prophet, saying, "He Himself took our infirmities and carried away our diseases." When you examine that scripture in Isaiah, you will find that by His scourging, we are healed! Because of Jesus, you don't have to live with disease, cancer, or sickness! I have seen cancer healed in Jesus' name.

I've watched many miracles, but I've also personally experienced them. I've laid my hands on a tumor and watched it shrink before my eyes as I spoke healing into it in the name of Jesus. I've done the same for a completely torn shoulder of one of my military teammates.

After praying, he immediately began performing one arm push-ups! I've watched God heal a torn quadriceps instantaneously when I prayed for it. The person I prayed for was supposed to be out of soccer for multiple weeks due to this already diagnosed injury. The person could barely walk and was on crutches. But after praying, she was running around the weight room where we had prayed! She went straight back to practice and performed great. She was completely healed!

One afternoon, an athlete approached me and asked me to pray for her shoulder. She was a softball player and had been struggling the past few weeks with pain while throwing the ball. It hadn't gotten better and she was really frustrated. Before praying, I had her move her shoulder around in a throwing motion. She winced as she moved it and said it "really hurt" to do that. I usually have people move an injured limb before praying for it, so that they know that God's healing is real and not a trick when the pain is gone. We then prayed together, and I commanded her shoulder to be healed in the name of Jesus.

After praying, I had her move her arm around again. Her face was astonished as she told me that she "felt no pain." I handed her a ball and told her to throw it as hard as she could. She gripped it, focused, and threw it with all of her might. She turned and looked back at me as her jaw dropped. Tears flooded her face as she came and sat down next to me.

"What's going on?" I asked.

Her words gave me goose bumps. "Why would Jesus do that for someone like me?"

She was completely healed and had no pain in her shoulder! She went back to softball practice and purposely demonstrated her healed throwing arm to the coach and shared her testimony of how Jesus had healed it.

These miracles occurred because there is power in the blood and name of Jesus! They occurred because of the covenant that we are under as children of God. God has also filled us with His Holy Spirit. The Bible says that the same spirit that raised Jesus from the dead lives in you! He didn't give you His Spirit for no reason. He clothed you with power so that He could work through you as His ambassador.

However, God doesn't meet your need—He meets your faith. Not everyone ran up to Jesus to get healed. But those who believed, who had faith, came up to Him and were healed every time. Jesus would say, "May it be done according to YOUR FAITH." It is by faith that we receive the promises we have as believers under the covenant.

If you step out in faith and you don't see the miracle right away, don't stop believing for it. God's promises are yes and amen and you will reap if you faint not. Continue to stand in faith and the promises under covenant will come. This covenant in Jesus' blood includes healing, prosperity, freedom, deliverance, protection, salvation, and victory in every area of your life.

Being a Christian doesn't mean you won't have trials in your life. What it means is that when they come, you have victory through your faith in Jesus! That's why "all things are possible to those that believe." That's why "In ALL these things we OVERWHELMINGLY conquer through Him who loved us"—Romans 8:37.

You aren't created for no reason. You are anointed by God as His ambassador to do His works on earth! You have been called and sent to do good and heal those oppressed of the devil. You can do all things through Christ who strengthens you!

But it won't happen magically or because you would like it to. You manifest your sonship when you exercise your faith. You must step into who you are and declare God's promises over your life. God's promises are for you but only if you believe in them, speak them, and become a doer of the Word!

These are only some of the blessings that God has for you in Christ. You could probably write a whole book on each of these areas, but I only touched on them to give you a foundation.

Chapter 2

WHY BE FIT?

You are probably asking the question of how fitness relates to all of what I just said! Well, I'm glad you asked. It is obvious now that you have an enormous anointing and call from God to advance His Kingdom. But are you prepared to not only meet that calling, but maximize it?

Your body is the platform by which you preach the gospel and perform everything that God has called you to do. You want to be physically fit so that you don't have any limits while fulfilling your calling. Your preparation in fitness ensures that you can participate in a task that requires physical fitness to accomplish. Your workouts are not pointless, but rather they enable you to reach out to people even more.

When you are physically fit, you will find that you have more energy throughout the day. You need this energy so that you can work hard, be a good example, and do the works that Jesus did! If you're not taking care of your body, then you won't have energy or the motivation to accomplish everything in the day that you need to.

What if your neighbor is in need of you performing a task that requires strength or endurance? Can you help take out the groceries out of the car with ease? Can you climb up on a roof, work all day, and help build a house for someone? Could you protect someone you love in a fight or catch the person who just stole your wife's purse? Could you walk around ALL day preaching like Jesus and his disciples did? Do you have the fitness you need to complete your day job to the BEST of your ability? So that when people look at you, they see someone who is serving by the strength that God supplies?

How can you share the gospel with everyone if you're tired after only working one hour? I want you to be able to rejoice in the strength and vitality that God has given you! Can God give you supernatural strength to accomplish a task? Absolutely! But you also reap what you sow and if you're not taking care of your body, then how can you expect to ask for energy miracles every day?

Before David ever killed Goliath, he had killed bears and lions. David wasn't a couch potato. He was physically fit and could defend his flock as a good shepherd. David knew if God was for Him, it didn't matter what was against him. But that knowledge didn't make David or his men not train.

In 1 Samuel chapter 30, we have the account of David returning with his men to their home in Ziklag. The city had been burned with fire, and the women and children taken captive! David strengthened himself in the Lord and decided to pursue the band of Amalekites that had conducted the raid. This was not an easy journey and a third of the men were left behind at the brook Besor. But David and 400 others continued the pursuit. Their workouts had enabled them to reach out.

They caught up to the band of Amalekites and slaughtered them from **twilight** until the **evening** of the **next day**. Could you imagine the physical endurance that it would take to endure such a long battle? Not one thing was missing and David's men recovered all of their wives, children, and possessions.

Could you participate in such a victory? What if all of the men were as the ones described as "too exhausted to follow"? You must take care of your body so that you are prepared to step into whatever task God needs you to accomplish! Even if you're not going on a grueling march like David and his men, there are still tasks that require your body to be physically fit.

Being physically fit helped me minister to my teammates in the military. As an infantryman, it's a requirement to be physically fit. Your fitness level can be the difference between life and death in a combat situation. If I wasn't physically fit, then it would reflect on me as being a poor soldier. As a Christian, you are constantly watched and observed. People are curious to see if there is anything real to your faith and the God you believe in. Being a poor soldier would hamper any attempts to preach Christ to my teammates.

I saw fitness as an opportunity to serve by the strength that God supplies. Fitness helped me become the distinguished honor graduate at basic training. You have to have a very high PT (physical training) score to do so. I preached Christ to many soldiers at basic, and this only solidified my testimony. Fitness helped me excel through airborne school and help other soldiers stay motivated.

After airborne school, I volunteered for Iraq and joined my unit down range. They had already been in Iraq for three months when I arrived. The situation meant that I would probably be looked at as a new private or "noob" who didn't know anything. A private who was excited about God and fighting for his country but who had no combat experience.

Within the first two weeks of me arriving, the unit conducted a PT test and a shooting test. I scored the highest in the company on the PT test and shot a perfect 40/40 on the M4 qualification (shooting test). Physical fitness had just opened up another door for me. Rather than being a noob, I was seen as a private with a lot of potential. I had gained instant respect and notoriety. Iraq became one of my greatest ministry fields. When faced with death, soldiers talk about God a lot. How could I reach them if I wasn't a good soldier myself? My workouts were enabling me to reach out.

That PT test was especially memorable due to the words spoken right before it. After I had maxed out my pushup and sit-up score, one of the SGTs asked me, "How do you think you will do on the run?" This SGT was built like a professional athlete and I had noticed his Ranger tab previously. Ranger school is one of the toughest schools in the military. It takes someone in excellent physical condition with a lot of heart to pass. I mentioned to the SGT that I "ran by the strength that God supplied" and spoke with confidence.

The SGT chuckled as he said, "God's got nothing to do with running. It's all about your legs." I countered back with, "Who made those legs?" Two seconds later the race started. I bolted out in a sprint, more motivated than I ever had been to win the 2-mile race and prove something to the Ranger. I could feel God strengthening me and my pace was quicker than normal.

As we turned around at the one-mile mark, the SGT was 50 meters ahead of me. I had run the first mile in 5:45 seconds, and somehow I had to find another gear. I dug deep and pushed. I passed the SGT with about a quarter mile left in the race and finished in first place! The victory that day led to constant conversation about God with that SGT and the rest of my teammates.

The everyday job in Iraq was very physical. We carried 30 pounds of body armor, our weapon, ammo, water, and backpacks. It usually added up to about 55 pounds of gear. Missions could last hours, and they included a lot of walking.

Walking sometimes turned into sprinting. My team leader and I sprinted to catch a truck that we suspected was bad news. We actually thought it may have contained a terrorist who had taken out one of our own a couple weeks back. We charged ahead of our squad to catch the truck, stop it, and pull the men out at gunpoint. Turns out they weren't the guys we were looking for and we let them go. That doesn't change the physical nature of the dead sprint to catch the truck!

Following Iraq, physical fitness continued to open doors for me. It helped me become soldier of the year for our battalion and later SGT of the year for our battalion. My whole unit knew I was a Christian and this once again helped solidify my testimony. There was evidence of God working in my life.

I couldn't have done anything in the military on my own. It is only through Christ that I was able to accomplish what I did. God will not let the righteous fall. He will never leave you or forsake you. If you stand up for Him, watch how He will bless you!

My experience in the military enabled me to pray with dozens of soldiers. I prayed with some of them to be saved, some to receive healing, some to be encouraged, some to be protected. I watched God perform instantaneous miracles through His Holy Spirit.

One of the soldiers couldn't put his rucksack on and was excluded from all assignments. He had a torn shoulder. He was completely healed on the spot and he asked to be filled with the Holy Spirit! God healed my teammate's hand, another's back, and another's knee. I watched God protect me again and again. In Iraq, my squad would have walked right on an IED if an Iraqi civilian had not reported it right before my platoon left for that exact location!

But would my experience in the military have been the same without physical fitness? Would I have accomplished the same things? Certainly not. I'm currently in my third year of teaching as a health and physical education teacher. Fitness is again opening doors. How can I be a good "gym teacher" if I'm not in shape? What kind of testimony would that be? Fitness allows me to play sports with the students and build a stronger rapport with them. Would I connect with them on the same level without it? Fitness gives me energy to serve God with all my might. It prevents sickness and disease and has enabled me to maximize my calling.

Your workouts will enable you to reach out as well. Even if your job isn't physical, there are many tasks in your life that are. Still not convinced that fitness is important? Keep reading.

TEMPLE OF THE HOLY SPIRIT

"Or do you not know that your body is a temple of the Holy Spirit who is in you, whom you have from God, and that you are not your own? For you have been bought with a price: therefore glorify God in your body."—1 Corinthians 6:19–20. We have God's Holy Spirit in us and our body is the temple in which that Spirit dwells. Jesus was very upset when He came to Jerusalem and found the temple of God being desecrated. He overturned the tables of the money changers and those who had made the temple of God a "robber's den."

How do you treat the temple that God has given you? Would Jesus be upset at the condition it is in? Your body should be built for God and fashioned for His purposes. Our bodies are a gift from God and we need to treat them that way. We should use these bodies to glorify God because they have been bought with precious blood!

"Yet the body is not for immorality, but for the Lord, and the Lord is for the body."—1 Corinthians 6:18. Our bodies should not look like sin or like the world. "Do you not know that your bodies are members of Christ? Shall I then take away the members of Christ and make them the members of a prostitute? May it never be!"—1 Corinthians 6:15. You don't want the temple of God's Spirit to be joined to a prostitute! Laziness, gluttony, overeating, and compromise are attacks of the enemy against your body. Don't join yourself or make a covenant with those things. You must take care of your temple and use it unto the glory of God!

A LIVING SACRIFICE

"Therefore I urge you, brethren, by the mercies of God, to present your bodies a living and holy sacrifice, acceptable to God, which is your spiritual service of worship."—Romans 12:1. We are to present our bodies as a sacrifice unto God. That means that your body, and everything you accomplish with your body, should be for the Lord and not for yourself.

When the Israelites presented a sacrifice, they would choose an animal that was unblemished and spotless. This animal would be the best of the flock, not one that was tainted. If we are walking as living sacrifices that are acceptable to God, then why taint our bodies by being unhealthy? Taking care of our bodies through physical fitness takes time, effort, and commitment. This dedication is not wasted, but is a sacrifice that is acceptable to God.

Walking in Victory

As a Christian, you can have victory in every area of your life. Do you look like someone walking in victory? You are constantly on display as a Christian. People should be able to see the joy of Christ in you and want to know where you got that joy from. They should be curious as to how you have so much energy, love, and happiness in your life.

2nd Corinthians 2:14 states, "But thanks be to God, who always leads us in triumph in Christ, and manifests through us the sweet aroma of the knowledge of Him in every place." You are walking in triumphal victory as a Christian. Everywhere you go, you are a carrier of God's presence. You are manifesting the "sweet aroma" of what it means to know God everywhere you go. Just like an aroma fills a room, the presence of God that you are carrying should fill the room and light up people's lives.

Paul says in 1 Corinthians 6:12 that, "I will not be mastered by anything." The only master you have is Jesus, and you can't serve two masters. You must not allow yourself to be held in bondage by laziness, obesity, unhealthy eating, or a lack of physical activity. Jesus has set you free from those things so why stay in bondage? By breaking the cycle, you will find yourself closer to God as you give your body solely unto Him. Not unto the world, not unto food, but solely for God.

In the Old Covenant, the Ark of the Covenant was carried on the shoulders of the Levitical priesthood. This was the only way it could be carried. When King David tries to bring the Ark of the Covenant to Jerusalem on an ox cart, the cart stumbles and the man who reaches out his hand to stabilize it dies. Only when David carries the ark the way God intended it to be—on the shoulders of the priesthood—does it come into Jerusalem in a display of praise and power.

Peter tells us in 1 Peter 2:9 that we are, "a chosen people, a royal priesthood." The presence of God is now carried on your shoulders just as it was in the days of King David. Your body is God's temple and you are a carrier of His presence wherever you go. Walk in victory! Let physical fitness be part of your testimony and newness of life. The spirit that God has given you is not defeat, it is not fear, but rather a spirit of power, love, and self-discipline (see 1 Timothy 1:7).

Rejoicing in How God Has Made You!

It's satisfying to walk in health and be able to do things with your body that you were created to! Psalm 139:14 states that, "I will give praise to You; for I am fearfully and wonderfully made." God has designed your body to do AMAZING things! Your body is a complex and miraculous creation that still boggles scientists. Acts 17:28 tells us, "In Him we live and move and exist." Notice that moving is part of truly living. God didn't design your body to sit still. He designed it for action. Being physically fit is a blessing and a reason to rejoice!

Preventing Disease and Sickness

Fitness is not just for professional athletes. Everyone can improve one's flexibility, cardiovascular endurance, muscular endurance, muscular strength, and body composition. These components are known as the "health-related components of physical fitness." These components will aid you in your daily life and will help prevent sickness and disease. So many people get sick due to a sedentary lifestyle!

While God can heal cancer and you can get a miracle through faith, why let sickness come in the first place? If you're speaking against cancer and yet you are living an unhealthy lifestyle, then are you really walking out your faith? Faith without works is dead, and people should be able to see your faith by your works (see the book of James). Fitness can prevent cancer, osteoporosis, cardiovascular disease, type II diabetes, stroke, depression, and high blood pressure!

Working out enables you to better reach out. Not that you couldn't reach out before, but now you are maximizing and extending your reach. Fitness gives you the energy to praise God at a whole new level. It opens up opportunities for you to witness and help others. It takes the limits off your body and allows you to do even more for God's kingdom. Sickness and disease flee from you, while benefits flow to you. You feel better, look better, and act better. You are taking care of the temple of the Holy Spirit that your body is. Offering your body up as a living sacrifice unto God. Freely moving and living in Christ and newness of life!

Chapter 3

A TRANSFORMED LIFE THROUGH A TRANSFORMED MIND

N ow that we understand why physical fitness is important to our walk with God, it's time to talk about how to achieve it! Don't worry about what condition you're currently in or your past experience. Your past has no future and won't help you. God is looking to see what you are going to do NOW and TODAY.

The Right Reasons

One of the biggest keys to becoming fit is identifying and correcting (if need be) your reason to become physically fit. If you want to get fit apart from God or for the wrong reasons, then you will find that you are separating yourself from God. Apart from God it will be harder to achieve fitness, and even if you do, it won't truly satisfy you. Psalm 127:1 states, "Unless the LORD builds the house, They labor in vain who build it."

Many people today want to become fit because of what society defines as an "ideal body image." Movies, commercials, magazines, and the internet portray this body image. Some people feel that they are "less of a person" if they don't think they look this way. This leads to a cycle of depression and effort to find acceptance by what others say is beautiful.

The "ideal body image" becomes an idol that people worship. They will do anything to achieve it because of the pleasure they think it will bring. But if you are pursuing an idol, it will only bring about death. There is only ONE God that you should be worshipping! Fitness is part of offering your body as a living sacrifice to Him, not to the world. You can't find your identity in your body composition. You are not defined by the world but by whom God says you are!

Your reason for becoming physically fit must be in sync with your walk with God. Don't let fitness become a gateway to sin or lustful obsession. Let fitness be a gateway to step you into your calling! Colossians 3:17 says, "Whatever you do in word or deed, do all in the name of the Lord Jesus, giving thanks through Him to God the Father." 1 Corinthians 10:31 states, "Whatever you do, do all to the glory of God." We should do everything unto the glory of God and in

His name! So if we are working out, then it must be done to His glory and not that of ourselves.

MINDSET ON WHAT GOD SAYS

A transformed life is impossible without a transformed mind. If you want to transform your body, then you first need to learn to control what you think and speak. If you don't believe you can do something, then you won't be able to! You won't have the confidence, effort, or dedication to achieve your goal. Nor will you take the steps of faith necessary to put your fitness transformation in process.

Let's take the man Jabez for example. You can find the short and remarkable account of Jabez in 1 Chronicles chapter 4. Starting at verse 9, "Jabez was more honorable than his brothers, and his mother named him Jabez saying, 'Because I bore him with pain.'" Now Jabez called on the God of Israel, saying, "Oh that You would bless me indeed and enlarge my border, and that Your hand might be with me, and that You would keep me from harm that it may not pain me!" And God granted him what he requested."

Here is a man who transformed his mind and transformed his words. Jabez's name means "sorrowful" or "painful." Jabez didn't accept that his life would be sorrowful. Rather, he specifically prayed that his life would not bring him pain or sorrow. He asked God to enlarge his border, protect Him, be with Him, and believed that God would change his destiny. He transformed his mindset and transformed his life.

If you want to successfully transform your physical body, then you have to believe you can do it. You have to line your words up with what God says about you just as Jabez did. It doesn't matter what people have called you in the past. It matters what you call yourself.

"We are destroying speculations and every lofty thing raised up against the knowledge of God, and we are taking every thought captive to the obedience of Christ."—2 Corinthians 10:5. You can't listen to negative thoughts or to negative words spoken by people. You must destroy those speculations and order your thoughts in God's Word.

Don't listen to the lies of the enemy that say you CAN'T. The devil will try and tell lies such as "You WON'T be able to get in shape. You CAN'T commit to something like that. You DON'T have the time. You're TOO TIRED to work out today. Exercise is TOO HARD. You're TOO OUT OF SHAPE to do anything about it. You are NOTHING." Don't listen to those lies or thoughts! What is important is what God's Word says about you! His Word declares that "you CAN do ALL things through Him who strengthens you."—Philippians 4:13.

Notice that the verse in Corinthians from the opening paragraph says the word "take." Changing your thoughts from what man says to what God says does not happen automatically. You must take those thoughts captive and line them up with the Word of God.

The devil is the father of lies and loves to lie to you! Since fitness is important to your walk with God, the devil will try and keep you bound in an unhealthy state of laziness, sickness, lies, depression, and negativity. Since the devil can't accuse you before God anymore, he will try and accuse you to yourself. When a negative thought or lie comes in, you must fight it! Praise God that He has given us the weapons we need to accomplish this!

WEAPONS OF WARFARE

You are not alone in fighting the good fight of faith. God has given you weapons more powerful than anything that would come against you. The key is to learn how to use them.

"For though we walk in the flesh, we do not war according to the flesh, for the weapons of our warfare are not of the flesh, but divinely powerful for the destruction of fortresses."—2 Corinthians 10:3–4. Let's break this verse down. When Paul says "flesh," he is talking about our physical body. Paul is stating that we have weapons for warfare that aren't of the flesh (or physical) but are spiritual in nature. Paul is talking about the weapons we have for spiritual warfare.

These weapons are "divinely powerful." The word translated as "divinely" in the NASB Bible is the Greek word *theos*, which can mean "the one true God, or godlike." The NKJ version of the Bible translates this word as "God" over 1,000 times in the Bible.

The word translated as "powerful" in the NASB Bible is the Greek word *dynatos*. This Greek word means "mighty, powerful, and possible." This is where Alfred Nobel got the word "dynamite" from. When we put these two words together, we see that the weapons of our warfare are Godlike in explosive and mighty power to make things possible and to tear down strongholds!

A stronghold can be a false mindset or anything the enemy has built up. You have the power in Christ to tear down every stronghold! This includes any strongholds that have prevented you from becoming physically fit in the past.

THE WORD AND YOUR WORDS

God's Word is one of the powerful weapons that you can use to tear down strongholds that have held you back from achieving your fitness goals. Instead of fighting battles in your mind by yourself, start battling them with what God says. To accomplish this, you need to spend time reading God's Word so that you know it. That way, when you feel sluggish or inadequate, you can start speaking scriptures and promises that God's Word says about you.

Allow me to share a quick story with you. From a young age, I prayed for a wife who would be excited about God. A wife who didn't just know of God, but who had a genuine relationship with

Him and was as passionate as I was about His kingdom. Well, God answered my prayers and then some! Not only did I find my perfect match in my wife Sandy, but her whole family was passionate about God! Her dad is the pastor of our church and walks with God closer than anyone I know. He is a pillar of faith and has had a tremendous impact on my life.

Our pastor has prayed for thousands of people and seen countless instantaneous miracles. One day, a tumor started growing on his neck. He was diagnosed with lymphoma by doctors. They said that he needed chemotherapy ASAP. I watched how Pastor battled this attack from the enemy. He didn't complain, he didn't feel sorrowful, he didn't listen to the report of the world. Instead, he listened to what God's Word said about him, and spoke it! He began to curse that cancer in Jesus' name and speak complete healing over it. He spoke scripture after scripture.

When Pastor returned to the doctor's office, he felt the cancer dissolve as he walked up the steps of the office! He went in the office weeping and began to praise God. The doctors were astonished. They marveled at the miracle that had occurred. When they ran tests, they couldn't find a single cancer cell in his body. It had completely disintegrated!

The Bible says that you speak what you believe. The more you say something, the more you believe it. Proverbs states that, "Death and life are in the tongue."—Proverbs 18:21. You can either speak life to your body, or you can speak death. James compares the tongue to the rudder of a ship. Though the tongue is small like a rudder of a ship, it is the guiding part of the whole body. It's time to turn your rudder to what God says about your body and sail into His plan for your life!

Are you a new Christian and don't know what promises to declare over your life? That's okay! God will accelerate you and reveal things to you as you begin reading His Word. Open up the Bible and personalize a passage of scripture or psalm for yourself.

In Jesus, we are under a "better covenant enacted on better promises."—Hebrews 8:6. That means that any blessings or promises given to the Israelites or men of God under the old covenant are blessings and promises for you, too! These blessings are not automatic, but come when you walk in covenant and relationship with God. Under Christ, we are now under EVEN BETTER promises! Search the scriptures and find what God says about His children. Then take what He says and start declaring it over your life. Job 22:28 tell us, "Decree a thing and it will be established."

Your words have power, but especially when you are speaking what God says. Hebrews 4:12 tells us that "The word of God is LIVING and ACTIVE and sharper than any two-edged sword, and piercing as far as the division of soul and spirit, of both joints and marrow, and able to judge the thoughts and intentions of the heart." God's Word is alive and powerful!

So what does division of the soul and spirit mean? You are a spirit, you live in a body, and you possess your soul. Your soul includes your mind, will, and emotions. You don't want to be led by your soul, but by your spirit. Speaking the Word of God allows you to accomplish this. The book of Romans tells us in chapter 8, "For all who are being led by the Spirit of God, these are sons of God." God's Word can judge the thoughts and intentions of your heart. When you listen to God's Word, you will start to align your will with God's will. You will begin to walk by His Spirit rather than impulsive or soulish thoughts.

With fitness, we don't want to have negative thoughts or words. You now know that God's Word is divinely powerful, that it tears down strongholds, that what you speak is important, and that you speak what you believe. So what are some scriptures from the Word of God that you can confess over yourself about fitness and health? Well, here you go! These are but a few:

Workout Confession Scriptures

- "Yet those who wait for the LORD will gain new strength; They will mount up with wings like eagles, They will run and not get tired, They will walk and not become weary." —Isaiah 40:31.
  - o Declare that you gain new strength in the Lord because you trust in Him. Muscles break down when you work them out so they need to rebuild or renew. Declare that your muscles renew in God. During your workout, declare that you don't get tired or weary but have strength to complete your session. Thank Him that you have endurance and are not sluggish. Watch how your energy level changes when you speak God's Word over yourself!
- "Therefore I run in such a way, as not without aim; I box in such a way, as not beating the air." —1 Corinthians 9:26.
  - o There is purpose to your workout! You have an aim, a goal, and are not just beating the air. Declare that your workout is for the purpose that God has for you.
- Declare Romans 12:1 over yourself, that your body is a "living sacrifice" unto God and you will take care of the temple that He gave you.
- Decree Colossians 3:17 over yourself that you will do everything (which includes your workout) unto the glory of God and in His name.
- "For by You I can run upon a troop; And by my God I can leap over a wall." —Psalm 18:29.
  - o Thank God that by Him you have strength to accomplish physical tasks.
- "Blessed be the LORD, my rock, Who trains my hands for war, And my fingers for battle." —Psalm 144:1. Psalm 18:34 states,

"He trains my hands for battle, So that my arms can bend a bow of bronze."

- o Thank God that you are trained up to handle whatever comes at you. You are trained in the spiritual and in the physical.
- "He Himself took our infirmities and carried away our diseases."—Matthew 8:17.
  - o Praise God as you declare that Jesus took away ALL of your sickness and disease. Command cardiovascular disease, cancer, arthritis (or any other sickness) to LEAVE in Jesus name."
- "And by His scourging we are healed."—Isaiah 53:5.
  - o Speak healing into your body in the name of Jesus. Command torn muscles, tendons, ligaments, and things out of order to come into order.
- "Let us run with endurance the race that is set before us."—Hebrews 12:1.
  - o We are called to fix our eyes on Jesus and to work hard for His kingdom. Declare that you have endurance to accomplish the tasks God has for you.
- "Therefore, strengthen the hands that are weak and the knees that are feeble, and make straight paths for your feet, so that the limb which is lame may not be put out of joint, but rather be healed."—Hebrews 12:12–13.
  - o Speak that anything in you that was weak is becoming strong and proficient.
- "Do you not know that those who run in a race all run, but only one receives the prize? Run in such a way that you may win."—1 Corinthians 9:24.
  - o Strive to be the BEST that you can be for God. (This includes giving your best in your workouts.)

- "For bodily discipline is only of little profit, but godliness is profitable for all things, since it holds promise for the present life and also for the life to come." — 1 Timothy 4:8.
  - o Fitness apart from God has very little profit. Sync your physical fitness with your walk with God since your relationship with Him is what is important. Remember, fitness apart from God can become an idol in an effort to find fulfillment through man instead of through God.
- "Finally be strong in the Lord and in the strength of His might." — Ephesians 6:10
  - o Thank God that your strength comes from Him.
- "The glory of young men is their strength." — Proverbs 20:29
  - o Rejoice in the strength that God has given you!

Chapter 4

FAITH AND FITNESS

I 've seen plenty of miracles, but this is one of my favorites. Coming out of college, and newly married, I was looking for a teaching position close to where I lived. Lots of people told me, "The economy is hard" or "Get ready to move far to find a teaching position."

Rather than listen to the naysayers, I stood in faith that God would provide and surrounded myself with people who would stand in faith with me. I knew my wife and I were called to stay in the area. June and July went by, and I had no job offers. August came around, and rather than panic, I kept standing in faith. Only two weeks before the school year started, I got a job interview with a school only ten minutes away from where I lived! This was a victory in itself.

The interview took place on a Thursday and went fantastic. The interview board told me that they would call me next week if I landed a second interview. Turns out the school called me the next day (which was a Friday). However, I didn't see the call and my old phone didn't show me when I had voicemail. Due to this, I didn't check my voicemail until Saturday.

Saturday afternoon, around 12:00 PM, I finally listen to the voicemail from the school. The voicemail tells me that I was supposed to call them back yesterday, on Friday, to setup an interview for Saturday morning. I realized I had already missed the scheduled time slot for the second interview! I quickly called the school but got messages saying that the school was closed until Monday. Had my phone just cost me a job? My competition probably interviewed all morning—did I just miss my opportunity? All kinds of negative thoughts began to flood my head as fear and anger attempted to grip me.

But instead of throwing a pity party, I began to combat those negative thoughts by praying in faith. I began to confess God's promises over myself. I paced around our apartment declaring scripture. I continued to call back the school, with the same voicemail messages telling me the school was closed. Around 2:00 PM, I decided to step out in faith and just believe God for a miracle. I put on a suit, didn't even know what building to go to, but decided to drive to the school anyway. I knew that with God all things are possible.

The first place I went was the District office. It looked like an empty parking lot, and thoughts tried to come in, saying, *Why did you put on a suit and drive out here, stupid?* But I trampled those thoughts with faith and decided to walk up to the door of the building anyway.

The first door to the building was open, and upon approaching the second door, a lady walked by and saw me. She unlocked the second door and asked who I was. Turns out there were two people in the building. They were the exact two people who I was supposed to have an interview with that morning! They interviewed me on the spot. Following the interview, one of the ladies told me, "We have interviewed all morning, but you're the one we want!" Praise God!

I could have let unbelief, fear, and anger stop me from walking into God's promise for me. The promise was there, I just had to literally **step out in faith** to go get it. God's Word tells us to "walk by faith" and that the righteous are to "live by faith." It tells us in Hebrews 11:6 that "without faith it is impossible to please Him, for he who comes to God must believe that He is and that He is a rewarder of those who seek Him." Ephesians 2:8 says that by grace we have been saved through faith.

If we are to walk by faith, live by faith, be saved through faith in Christ, and please God through faith, then faith is obviously EXTREMELY IMPORTANT to your walk as a Christian! In fact, the disciples of Jesus were disciples of faith. Jesus was teaching them how to move and operate in this spiritual law. You can see this in the book of Matthew, where Jesus constantly teaches on faith and demonstrates it. And yes, as you're probably guessing by now, faith is a very important key to becoming physically fit.

Let's look at the Hebrews 11:6 verse about pleasing God through faith. Notice that you must believe that God is real and that He rewards those who seek Him. Since God rewards those who seek Him, then you can't have a false mindset or stronghold that says, "Fitness and good health aren't for you." You can't believe a lie that you won't be able to become physically fit or that it's good to suffer in unhealthiness.

God doesn't have any sickness, isn't the author of it, didn't create mankind with it, and doesn't want you to have it either. Since you're in a fallen world, you'll be attacked by things (as everyone is), but the difference as a Christian is that you have power through faith in Christ to break it off you. God wants you to be in good health!

The apostle John states that, "Beloved, I pray that in all respects you may prosper and be in **good health**, just as your soul prospers."—3 John 1:2. God wants you whole and blessed "in all respects," and this includes your health. Have faith that God WILL reward you when you seek Him and put Him first in your life! "But seek first His kingdom and His righteousness, and all these things will be added to you."—Matthew 6:33.

Okay, so we understand that by faith we believe that God is a rewarder of those who seek Him, and that He IS. He isn't dead, isn't far off, but IS, and IS the same God yesterday, today, and forever. But what is faith exactly? We know we need it to please God, but what is it?

Hebrews 11:1 defines faith for us. This verse states, "Now faith is the assurance of things hoped for, the conviction of things not seen." Looking at a different translation of the same verse, the NKJV says, "Now faith is the substance of things hoped for, the evidence of things not seen."

Notice that both translations start with the phrase, "Now faith is." Faith is not something that you should do tomorrow, or when you're a better Christian, but something you should do right NOW! Faith requires action. If you truly believe something, then your words, actions, and fruit should line up with what you say. James says that "faith without works is dead."—James 2:26.

Taking care of your body and becoming physically fit isn't something for the future, it's for right NOW. If you truly believe that all things are possible with God, and that you can do all things through Him, then take a step of faith and MOVE! Step into action not next year, not after dessert, but right now.

You don't have to wait until tomorrow for God to use you. God doesn't dwell in time, He dwells in the NOW because he always was, always is, and always will be. He is calling His sons and daughters to step out in faith and do His works on earth. He is looking for people who don't walk by what they see, but step out in a NOW moment.

The second part of the verse in Hebrews states that faith is the "assurance of things hoped for" or the "substance of things hoped for." Faith is different from hope. God doesn't want you to "hope" He is real or that His promises are real. He wants you to believe and have faith. Assurance denotes a complete confidence. You are sure in what God's Word says, not back and forth. A "substance" is something that is tangible and real.

Your faith should be the same way. Since you walk by faith and not by sight, there should be a tangible response to what you know to be true even if you can't see it. Instead of "seeing to believe," you need to flip it and believe to see! "While we look not at the things which are seen, but at the things which are not seen; for the things which are seen are temporal, but the things which are not seen are eternal." — 2 Corinthians 4:18.

Since fitness is important to your walk as a Christian, it's time to walk by faith and believe that you can achieve it. You CAN take care of the temple God gave you. You CAN offer your body as a living sacrifice unto Him. You CAN use your body as the vessel by which to spread the gospel. You CAN prosper in health as your soul prospers. You CAN be healed, renewed with energy, and filled with strength. You CAN be equipped and ready to accomplish physical tasks for God's kingdom! Stand in faith on all of the promises that God has for you when you are in covenant with Him!

PRAYING IN FAITH

"The effective prayer of a righteous man can accomplish much." –James 5:16. Why do you think the word "effective" is contained in this verse? Are some prayers not as effective? The answer is YES! Remember, God meets your faith, not your need. Mixing doubt and unbelief with your prayers can negate the promises that you had coming your way!

In Matthew 13, we see Jesus "not do many miracles there because of their unbelief." The city of Nazareth didn't believe in Jesus because they had become too familiar with Him. Nazareth was Jesus' hometown, and they were blinded that the carpenter they knew could somehow be the Messiah. If you study out the account of this story in Mark 6, you see that the few people who did receive a miracle were the deaf and the mute. The people who couldn't hear the message of unbelief, and believed themselves, were the ones who received a miracle!

In Luke chapter 4, we see Jesus tell the people that there were many lepers and widows in the days of Elijah and Elisha but that Elijah was only sent to the widow Zarephath and that only Naaman the leper was cleansed. Zarephath and Naaman received their miracles because they stepped out in faith! We can read their stories in the book of Kings.

You speak what you believe. If you are truly standing in faith on God's promises for your health, and that you can do all things through Christ (including taking care of your body), then your prayer language should echo that.

James talks about the danger of mixing in unbelief and doubt into your prayers. In reference to asking God for wisdom, James says, "But he must ask in faith without any doubting, for the one who doubts is like the surf of the sea, driven and tossed by the wind. For that man ought not to expect that he will receive anything from the Lord, being a double-minded man, unstable in all his ways."—James 1:6–8. The word for *double-minded* also means "doubting" or "hesitating." Don't let doubt or unbelief creep in and negate the effectiveness of your prayer.

What does Jesus say about praying in faith? In Mark 11, Jesus tells us, "Have faith in God. Truly I say to you, whoever says to this mountain, 'Be taken up and cast into the sea,' and does not doubt in his heart, but **believes that what he says is going to happen**, it **will** be granted him. Therefore I say to you, **all things** for which you pray and ask, believe that you have received them, and they will be granted to you."

This is a very powerful passage of scripture! Mountains aren't just physical. Being overweight, obese, unhealthy, or having a lack of energy can be a mountain that is raised up against you; a high obstacle that is in the way of your calling. But you can cast that mountain into the sea! You can stand in faith, not doubting, and it WILL be granted to you. Jesus doesn't say to have faith in some things you pray for, but for ALL things for which you pray or ask. Begin to thank God that you WILL be fit for His calling. Thank Him for His anointing and declare that you can overwhelmingly conquer all things through Christ who strengthens you (see Romans 8:37).

You may be thinking, "Well if I can ask for anything and receive it, then couldn't I ask to fly like Superman, bench 5,000 pounds, turn invisible when I want, shoot flaming rockets out of my hands, and be the king of the world for the rest of my life?" You find the answer to this question in 1 John chapter five.

John says, "This is the confidence which we have before Him, that if we ask anything according to His will, He hears us. And if we know that He hears us in whatever we ask, we know that we have the requests which we have asked from Him." So when you pray or ask for something in God's will, you know that you have it and can stand in faith. That is different from praying for worldly, selfish, or sinful things. This raises the question, "Well how do I know what God's will is?"

You know His will by His Word. God is the same yesterday, today, and forever. He is unchanging. What Jesus' will was back then, it still is now. It is God's will for you to be healed, delivered, protected, saved, redeemed, made righteous, clothed with power, made prosperous, and sent out into the world as His Son was sent! It is His will for you to do the works that Jesus did, to advance His kingdom, spread His gospel, and to bring Him glory. You can stand in faith on the promises that God has given you through His Word. "For as many as are the promises of God, in Him they are yes; therefore also through Him is our Amen to the glory of God through us."—1 Corinthians 1:20.

On top of His Word, God has given you His Spirit. His Spirit teaches you all things, searches even the depths of God, and reveals His will to you. The more you are led by the Spirit, and not by your flesh, the more your will is going to line up with God's will. Too many Christians don't realize that they have the ability to know God's will. They add the tag phrase, "If God wills" to every statement that they say.

This tag phrase takes the pressure off their prayers, since if it doesn't happen, then they assume it just wasn't God's will. If God has already told you that something IS HIS WILL, then don't question it. That is where doubt and unbelief sneak in again. Get your prayer language in line with God's Word and you will see supernatural miracles begin to be abundant in your life!

HOW TO BUILD FAITH

Perhaps you are thinking, "Well I want to have faith but I don't know how?" Romans 10:17 states, "So faith comes from hearing, and hearing by the word of Christ." You grow in faith when you read God's Word. The more you read it and speak it, the more it is written on your heart. You will begin to be led by God's Word and not by what the world tells you. Now you can "take up the shield of faith, with which you can extinguish all the flaming missiles of the evil one."—Ephesians 6:16. By faith you can destroy every attack of the enemy against you!

How can you have faith in God's Word and promises for your life if you don't know it? Let yourself be a "hearer" of the Word and then put action to what you know and become a "doer" of the Word. If you don't apply what you have heard, then you are just building a house on sand that will be washed away when the waves come in.

To grow your faith, you need to apply it and "use your faith on purpose." For example, let's say that you own a really nice car. You only get use out of your car if you drive it. Your car doesn't benefit you to just sit in your garage. Your faith won't grow if you leave it sitting in a garage. You need to start using it ON PURPOSE in your life. It's not enough to listen to the sound of the engine. You must push your foot down on the pedal and start driving!

In Luke 17, upon hearing how often they should forgive their brother, the disciples tell Jesus, "Increase our faith!" Instead of increasing their faith on the spot, Jesus reveals how they can grow and develop it. Jesus tells them, "If you had faith like a mustard seed, you would say to this mulberry tree, 'Be uprooted and be planted in the sea' and it would obey you."—Luke 17:6. Matthew 13 shows us that while a mustard seed is very small, it can grow up larger than other garden plants. However, to accomplish this, it must be sown in good soil, watered, and taken care of.

Jesus is letting His disciples know that their faith can grow and develop into great faith just as the mustard seed grows. To accomplish this, you must put yourself in good soil (surround yourself with good fellowship), be constantly nourished (the Word of God and prayer), and remove thorns from around you.

A seed doesn't do you any good if you keep it hidden away in your pocket. You must USE your faith on purpose! The more you "use your faith," the more you will see God answer your faith. "For the eyes of the LORD move to and fro throughout the earth that He may strongly support those whose heart is completely His."—2 Chronicles 16:9. God is searching for sons and daughters that He can strongly support! God will meet your faith, and your faith will grow as you see His miraculous power in your life.

Relationship

James 4: 8 states, "Draw near to God and He will draw near to you." The more you seek God, the more you will find Him. As you grow in your relationship with God, your faith will be strengthened, and your doubts will be starved to death. Jesus often went off by Himself to pray. He constantly spent time with our Father in Heaven. Due to this, whenever a trail or circumstance confronted Jesus, He responded in faith. We see this in the garden of Gethsemane. Jesus told His disciples to pray, but they kept falling asleep while Jesus prayed. When the soldiers came to take Jesus, He responded in faith while the disciples reacted in fear.

God wants to have a close relationship with you! He created you, loves you, and desires that you seek Him above all else. Your relationship with God will strengthen your faith and give you direction, wisdom, revelation, and the ability to move in power and demonstration of His Spirit. You can't expect to do great things with God if you don't spend time with Him! He is the root and you're only a branch. Apart from Him you can do nothing. But when you let that root fill you with living water, you will be able to pour out victory into every area of your life including fitness!

Stand in faith on God's promises for your health and fitness. I think that the number one reason people don't achieve fitness is because they give up. Doubts and obstacles came in and broke the progress. If you stay consistent, you will get results.

Believe you can achieve a healthy body. Believe for strength in your workouts, success in your goals, and the energy you need to advance God's kingdom. Use your faith on purpose, speak God's Word, grow in it, and let that faith motivate you to push yourself harder than you ever have before! God already said you can do all things through Him. What are your waiting for? Grab that promise for yourself, speak it and believe it.

Chapter 5

PHYSICALLY FIT PEOPLE IN THE BIBLE

Taking care of your body for God is not a new principle. I've already went into many of the scriptures that instruct a believer to be fit. But were there any people in the Bible who actually applied this principle? Absolutely! In fact, it goes all the way back to the beginning.

When God created Adam and Eve, He created them in His image and after His likeness. They didn't have disease, sickness, pain, fear, or sin. Adam and Eve were probably very fit. They were created with a healthy body meant to MOVE! Acts 17:28 tells us that "in Him we live and move and exist."

Adam and Eve weren't created with a body that would hinder them. They were full of energy, full of life, and able to perform physical tasks. They were instructed by God to "be fruitful and multiply, and fill the earth, and subdue it; and rule over the fish of the sea and over the birds of the sky and over every living thing that moves on the earth."—Genesis 1:26. You can't rule over God's creation by sitting down all day! Adam and Eve did not live a sedentary lifestyle.

Adam and Eve also had good food to eat. Their food was not filled with preservatives, extra sugar, or extra fat. On top of all of this, sin had not come into the world yet. Adam and Eve didn't have to worry about things that could have a negative impact on their body. They only had to avoid the one tree that God told them not to eat from.

After the Fall, mankind continued to live a very physically active lifestyle. Families back then could not go to the grocery store and get all the food they needed to survive. They had to physically work for it! When God addressed Adam and Eve after the Fall, he told Adam, "Cursed is the ground because of you; In toil you shall eat of it all the days of your life. Both thorns and thistles it shall grow for you; And you shall eat the plants of the field; by the sweat of your face you shall eat bread."—Genesis 3:18. People had to be physically active in order to farm, raise livestock, shepherd animals, hunt, build shelter, and survive.

Whether you look in the New Testament or the Old Testament, you will find great men of faith who were also warriors. To name just a few, take your pick: from Joshua, Caleb, Gideon, Ehud, David, Cornelius in Acts, the centurion that Jesus talked to, or even God Himself who is described as a victorious warrior! As an infantry sergeant, I knew physical fitness was essential to my job as a warrior. The more my unit sweated in training, the less likely we would bleed in war. Fitness was important to the warriors of the Bible as well.

Take Abraham for example. In Genesis 14, Abraham's nephew Lot is taken captive by an army made up of four different kings. This army was likely thousands in number. And yet Abraham, who believes that God is with him, decides to attack this army by night with only 318 men! God is with Abraham and, by stepping out in faith, he defeats the army of kings and retrieves his nephew Lot. Verse 14 of this chapter reveals that these 318 men were trained for combat. If God is for you, it doesn't matter who is against you; but that doesn't mean that you don't train! These men were physically fit warriors who stepped out in faith and believed God along with Abraham for victory.

Abraham was used to long journeys on foot so it wasn't hard to track down the kings who took Lot. Abraham was not born in the land of Canaan, but journeyed there in obedience to God's voice from the land of Ur of the Chaldeans. Abraham probably journeyed about 900 miles in the path he took to get from modern day Iraq to the Promised Land!

King David was a mighty warrior and was very physically active. Even while a youth, David possessed the strength and agility to kill lions, bears, and whatever was a threat to the sheep he was watching. He led Israel in many battles so that the people chanted that he had killed "ten thousands" of the enemy.

David maximized his physical strength due to his faith in God. David states in Psalm 18, "For who is God, but the Lord? The God who **girds me with strength**, and makes my way blameless? He makes **my feet like hinds feet**, and sets me upon my high places. **He trains my hands for battle**, so that **my arms can bend a bow of bronze**." Earlier in this Psalm, David says, "For by Thee **I can run upon a troop; And by my God I can leap over a wall**."

Whether it was strength to bend a bow, speed to run like a hind, endurance to run upon a troop, or power to jump over a wall, all of these physical characteristics were maximized from David's relationship with God. Jesus didn't come to CHANGE who you are but to REDEEM who you are. David's gifts and talents, including his fitness, were blessed due to this relationship.

David had an elite group of "mighty men." These men have their names recorded in 2 Samuel chapter 23. They accomplished amazing acts of valor! One of them killed 800 at one time. Another ran like a gazelle. Another stood his ground in the middle of a field and defended it while the rest of the army of Israel fled (he then turned the tide and Israel won the battle). Three of the mighty men attacked a whole garrison of the Philistines by themselves just to bring

David water! The mighty men even helped kill off giants that were the sons of Goliath (see 2 Samuel 21:15–22).

Swinging a sword around for a few minutes can get pretty tiring. How many times do you think you would have to swing it to kill 800 men at one time? These men did amazing physical feats in battle. Once again, it came down to their relationship with God. These men were once people who were either in distress or in debt. But they came down to David at the cave of Adullam and decided to follow him (see 1 Samuel 1–2). They submitted to the leadership of someone who earnestly sought God and who lived by faith. God redeemed who they were and now they are listed as some of the greatest warriors who ever lived!

Have you ever thought about how much walking Jesus did with his disciples? Some of the disciples who followed Jesus were probably already fit in the first place. Those of them who were fishermen (such as John, James, and Peter) lived a very active lifestyle.

It takes a lot of effort to take a boat out to sea, haul in a catch with nets, bring that catch back to shore, and then go back out to do it all again. Following the King of kings meant walking miles and miles in-between cities. Besides preaching from city to city, Jesus and His disciples would journey to Jerusalem multiple times a year for feasts. In your current shape, would you have been able to follow Jesus? Fitness was important back then, and it's just as important now.

SUPERNATURAL ACTS OF PHYSICAL FITNESS

It's important to be physically fit so that you can fully live out the calling that God has for you. But regardless of your current level of fitness, God can give you strength or endurance supernaturally to accomplish something for His name. This isn't a license to not be physically fit. You shouldn't have to believe God for a miracle everyday just to accomplish daily physical tasks. However, it's also important to know that you are not limited to your current state of fitness and that God can do mighty things through you right now.

Take Samson, for example. Samson was called to deliver Israel from the Philistines. Samson possessed supernatural strength due to His covenant with God as part of the Nazarite vow. He was able to tear apart a lion with his bare hands, kill a thousand men with a donkey's jawbone, and pull out and carry the gates of a city!

When Samson broke the law of the Nazarite and his hair was cut deceitfully by Delilah, "his strength left him." As his hair began to grow, his strength began to return. Samson prayed for great strength to bring down the house where he was being mocked by the Philistines and God gave it to him. Samson killed more people in his death by bringing this house down than he had killed during his life, and he delivered Israel from the Philistines. We see that Samson possessed supernatural strength, and that this strength was attached to his covenant and vow to God.

Another example of God strengthening someone supernaturally is found when Elijah outran Ahab's chariot. "And Ahab rode and went to Jezreel. Then the **hand of the Lord was on Elijah,** and he girded up his loins and **outran** Ahab to Jezreel." It was a 17-mile run from Mt. Carmel to Jezreel. Many versions of the Bible translate this passage of scripture as having Elijah running before Ahab's chariot instead of outrunning it. Whether Elijah outran the chariot, or ran the same speed as the chariot, it is a noteworthy physical accomplishment!

Strive to get in the best shape that you can for God, but don't limit yourself while you work to achieve this. God can supernaturally work through you right now to advance His kingdom. You don't have to wait to achieve a certain standard. Start moving now, start living for Him now, and He will move in turn on your behalf.

Fitness Vocabulary

To fully understand the principles of physical fitness, training methods, and workout routines, you should have a foundation on some common vocabulary terms. As a physical education teacher, vocabulary is one of the first things I teach at the start of each new unit. How can you grasp a concept if you don't understand the terminology in the explanation of that concept? Here are some common vocabulary terms used in the field of physical fitness.

- **Health-related components of physical fitness**: These components are areas of your health that are improved through physical activity. They include cardiorespiratory endurance, muscular strength, muscular endurance, flexibility, and body composition.
- **Cardiorespiratory/cardiovascular endurance**: The term "endurance" refers to how long you can perform a given exercise over a period of time. Cardiorespiratory/cardiovascular endurance is the ability of the heart and lungs to supply oxygenated blood and fuel to your muscles and body tissues during exercise.
- This component of your health can be increased by any physical activity that increases your heart rate (especially those that elevate your heart rate for an extended duration). Cardiovascular refers more to your heart while cardiorespiratory refers more to your lungs (they go hand in hand with each other).
- **Muscular strength**: The maximal amount of force that a muscle can produce.
- **Muscular endurance**: The ability of a muscle to exert itself or perform multiple contractions over an extended period of time.
- **Flexibility**: The ability to move a joint and its corresponding muscles and body parts through a full range of motion.

- **Body composition**: This is the percentage of your body fat compared to your lean body tissue.
- **Skill-related components of physical fitness**: These components are specific skills that physical fitness may improve. These skills are specific to certain activities and sports. Some activities will increase these components more than others, or focus on a certain component more than other activities. These components include speed, power, agility, balance, and coordination.
  - o **Speed**: The time it takes for your body to accomplish a given movement.
  - o **Power**: the ability of your body to rapidly move with explosive force.
  - o **Agility**: the ability of the body to quickly change direction during movement.
  - o **Balance**: The ability of the body to maintain equilibrium.
  - o **Coordination**: The ability of your body to perform multiple motor skills at the same time.
- **Muscle Fiber Type**: Your body is mainly composed of two different types of muscle fiber known as either Type I or Type II muscle fiber. There are a few other muscle fiber types but I will focus on the two main types for this book. You are born with a certain percentage of each muscle fiber type. However, research has shown that training may have a big influence on changing these percentages in your body.

Each muscle fiber type has different advantages and disadvantages. Due to this, it is important to tailor your training towards the type of muscle fiber you want your body to be composed of. Elite athletes have a very high percentage of the muscle fiber that benefits their particular sport. These percentages can be as high as 80 percent for one fiber type and 20 percent for the other type.

The average person or an athlete who cross trains will have a more balanced ratio. While muscle fiber type is only a small aspect of obtaining peak performance, it can make the difference when performing at an elite level.

Have you ever looked at a delicious cooked turkey on Thanksgiving Day? You probably have noticed that the turkey is comprised of both white and dark meat. The white meat is Type I muscle fiber. The dark meat is Type II muscle fiber. Your body is broken up into these muscle fiber types just like the turkey.

- **Type I muscle fiber**: This fiber type has a very high aerobic endurance. It is very efficient at continuing to produce energy through the oxidation of carbohydrates and fat while you are exercising. This fiber type is great for endurance athletes such as cross-country runners, bikers, and long distance swimmers.

Your muscles won't get fatigued as fast and you will be able to perform at a moderate intensity for an extended duration. However, this muscle fiber type is not built for power or speed. Type I muscle fibers are connected to smaller motor neurons than Type II muscle fibers (producing less power). They also have a very slow contraction speed (slow-twitch muscle fiber). Due to this, they can't contract with the same amount of force as type II muscle fibers since they can't contract as rapidly.

- **Type II muscle fiber**: These muscle fibers are known as "fast-twitch" and can contract/fire rapidly. This allows them to contract more frequently than Type I fibers and produce more force. Type II muscle fibers are great for power, strength, and speed. You will find a high percentage of these fibers in football players, weight lifters, and sprinters.

Type II muscle fibers are connected to large motor neurons that contain more fibers compared to the small motor neurons containing type I muscle fibers. This allows for more fibers to be contracted by each neuron and leads to an increase in strength. However these fibers are built for anaerobic exercise and fatigue quickly. They will get tired more easily than type I muscle fibers.

- **Aerobic exercise**: The word "aerobic" means "in the presence of oxygen"—(Wilmore 40). Aerobic exercise is prolonged exercise that needs oxygen to continually function. This type of exercise is characterized by endurance activities that last for an extended period of time.
- **Anaerobic exercise**: This type of exercise is characterized by short and intense bursts of activity. Anaerobic exercise is performed without oxygen and utilizes energy from other sources such as the PCr (Phosphocreatine) system. This type of exercise is used for a short sprint, a set of pushups, or a play in football.
- **Concentric contraction**: When a muscle shortens
- **Eccentric contraction**: When a muscle lengthens
- **Metabolism**: The ability of the body to convert food into energy. Your metabolism can be increased through physical activity. One of the biggest keys to weight loss is increasing your metabolism through exercise. Muscle is more metabolically active than other body tissues. This means that it takes more energy to continually function. If you increase your ratio of muscle to fat in your body, you will increase the amount of

energy that your body must burn to maintain equilibrium. This can lead to an increase in your resting metabolic rate (RMR).

RMR is the amount of calories that you burn "at rest" while you are not exercising. High intensity exercise has also been found to keep your metabolism at an elevated rate for a prolonged period after you exercise (due to EPOC, removing lactate from your body, and returning the body to homeostasis).

In this chapter, we looked through the Bible and saw many men and women of God who were physically fit. Whether it was Adam and Eve, Abraham, David, Joshua, Samson, the mighty men, or Jesus' disciples. Fitness enabled these people to maximize the calling that God had on their lives. Fitness was important then, and it is important now.

You have also learned the fitness vocabulary necessary to understand the next sections of this book. You are now ready to dive into some training and workout principles! These principles are vital in any workout routine, including your own.

Chapter 6

WORKOUT PRINCIPLES

There are many different thoughts and ideas on workout routines, types of workouts, and the most effective ways to become physically fit. In your own life, you have probably heard some good advice, and you have probably heard some really bad advice. How do you sort through all of this information to find the truth?

Regardless of the specifics of your perfect workout, there are proven fitness principles that are true no matter what type of workout you are doing. Mastering these principles is essential in maximizing the efficiency of your workout. Maximize your workouts to maximize your reach out. Not surprisingly, many of these fitness principles are also spiritual truths that line up with the Word of God.

THE PRINCIPLE OF OVERLOAD

For your muscles to get stronger, you have to "overload" them. This means that you have to load them up or exert your muscles more than they are used to. God has given your body the ability to get stronger to meet demands placed upon it.

For example, when you lift weights, you are pushing against more resistance than your body would be without the weights. Your body recruits muscle fibers to meet this challenge. These fibers are torn and broken apart during the overloaded exertion. The harder the strain to lift the weight, or the longer the strain on your muscles, the more broken down the fibers in your muscle become.

The body will then rebuild these muscle fibers back stronger to meet future demands. Your muscle fiber size can increase (known as muscular hypertrophy) or your body may become more efficient at recruiting your muscle fibers. Once your body has adapted to lifting a higher weight, you will have to increase the weight amount or the amount of repetitions to cause your body to be overloaded again.

If you don't work out hard and truly overload your muscles, they will never get stronger. The same principle is true for a workout focusing on cardio or muscular endurance. The farther, harder, and longer you perform the activity, the greater the change will be in your body to meet that task in the future. You have to work to get to the next level.

If you are not very physically active, you may see rapid growth and increase through your workouts. If you are a seasoned athlete and already possess a high level of physical fitness, then you will have to work even harder to overload your body to achieve a new level.

The overload principle is one of the reasons a spotter or workout partner is so important. They can push you harder than you might push yourself. During an exercise, they can also help you just enough to keep on lifting past muscular failure. This technique allows you to overload your muscles more than on your own.

The same overload principle is true in your spiritual walk. If you want to increase your walk or relationship with God, then you need to seek Him MORE than you have been. Have you plateaued as a Christian? Are you on fire for God or are you beginning to become lukewarm? God has so much for you to step into but it takes action on your part! If you want to look more like Christ, then you need to spend more time with Him. If you're having trouble with this, then get someone to keep you accountable and encourage you just like the spotter in the gym.

The disciples followed Jesus everywhere. Their relationship with Him allowed them to step into the power and anointing that God had on their lives. If you want to operate in that kind of anointing, then you have to SEEK God like they did. You have to OVERLOAD yourself and seek God more than you are used to. "But from there you will seek the LORD your God, and you will find Him if you search for Him with all your heart and all your soul." —Deut 4:29.

The Principle of Rest/Recovery

So how often do you need to rest? This is a largely debated topic. The recovery time you need depends on a few different variables. It depends on the intensity, type, and length of your workouts. It also depends on the person's ability to recover and one's current fitness level.

If you are new to working out, you should start off working out three to four times a week. Working out too hard after living a sedentary lifestyle could lead to injury. After you have gotten used to this for a few weeks, you can gradually increase the amount of training days.

No matter what training regimen you are following, you should have a complete day of rest at least once per week. If you are doing more of a cardio program (consisting of aerobic activities such as biking, swimming, or running), then you can do the same training up to five to six times a week. However, it is often beneficial to vary the intensity of these workouts (or change the type of activity).

Cardio activities are often known as "aerobic" activities. This means that your muscles are using oxygen to operate over an extended period of time. These activities focus on building cardiovascular endurance and muscular endurance. They do not break down your muscle fibers as much as an activity focused on building muscular strength (such as weight training). Due to this, you can perform these workouts more often without overtraining.

If you are performing an activity that builds muscular strength, then you need to give your muscles additional recovery time to build back stronger. If a tornado were to hit a house, the people in the house would need some time to rebuild it. They couldn't rebuild the house if a tornado hit their house three times a day. How much recovery time you need depends on how broken down your muscles are along with your body type.

If you completely exhaust a muscle group, then most researchers suggest allowing forty-eight hours for that muscle group to recover before working it out again. This is why many people vary what muscle groups they work on (so that they can still work out every day).

For example, you could do biceps/triceps on Monday, legs on Tuesday, chest/shoulders/back on Wednesday, abs/cardio on Thursday, full body workout on Friday, speed workout Saturday, and rest on Sunday. Notice that this workout plan doesn't exhaust the same muscle groups two days in a row. Whatever muscle group is exhausted builds back while you are exhausting a different muscle group. For workouts that tailor towards muscular strength and are heavy in weight, seventy-two hours of rest is recommended.

Does this mean that you can't lift the same muscle group a few days in a row? Not necessarily. In fact, one of the ways to prevent plateauing is to completely exhaust a muscle group a few days in a row, take a rest day, and then do it again. This is done with low weights to prevent injury. Follow this routine for two to three weeks. Keep performing your normal routine and rotation during these weeks, just hit the target muscle group sometime later in the day (high reps low weight) for three out of four nights.

After the two to three weeks, go back to your normal routine where you were only lifting this muscle group every few days. Due to the enormous strain you've put on the target muscle group, you may experience accelerated growth over the next few weeks since your body has an opportunity to build to meet a similar demand. Notice that even in this approach, there is still a rest/recovery period.

The time needed for your muscles to recover also depends on the way God has made you and your current fitness level. Some people seem to recover quicker than others. This could be due to the way they were created, or due to their training.

Seasoned athletes recover a lot quicker and can perform vigorous physical activity daily. They have pushed their body to an elite level that maximizes the benefits of working out. There are even some Olympic lifters that work out four to six hours every day and lift the SAME muscle groups!

Conventional thinking would call this crazy, but they get stronger nonetheless. On the other hand, there are Olympic lifters who purposely spread out their workout (or have variety to it) to allow time for muscular growth.

For me personally, I seem to see the best results in strength gains by lifting each body part twice a week. For example, chest/

back/shoulders on Monday and Friday, legs/abs on Tuesday and Thursday, biceps/triceps on Wednesday and Saturday. This allows ample time for each muscle to fully recover to its maximum potential before being broken down again. You can throw in your sprint/ cardio workouts on top of your strength training. Your muscles aren't fatigued as much from them. Below is a modified chart based off information in the ACE Personal Trainer Manual for recommended amounts of rest based upon the activity.

Activity	Rest Intervals during Workout	Amount of Rest after workout
Aerobic low intensity cardio	≥ 20 minutes	24 hours
Anaerobic high intensity	≤ 5 minutes	24–48 hours
Muscular strength	2–5 minutes	72 hours
Muscular endurance	1–2 minutes ≤ 30–60 seconds high intensity	48 hours
Muscular hypertrophy	30–90 seconds	48 hours–72 hours
Power	2–5 minutes	48–72 hours

Sleep

The most important aspect of rest is getting enough sleep each night! Sleep helps your body stay in equilibrium. It aids in the proper function of your entire body. If you negate sleep, you will likely hold on to more fat. Most people who stay up late end up eating additional food. This food outweighs any benefit of calories burned by being awake.

Due to lack of sleep, your body will crave carbohydrates and more food. Not to mention your metabolism and hormones are regulated by your sleep. Sleep is essential to maximizing the release of the hormones that build muscle.

Lack of sleep can lead to a decreased metabolism. If your metabolism is low, you won't burn as many calories during the day, and you will negate any efforts to lose weight. You need sleep to have the energy necessary to fully maximize your workouts. Without rest, the overall function of your body will decrease and lead to significant health issues.

Head Coach Chip Kelly of the Philadelphia Eagles knows how important sleep is. He recommends that his athletes get ten to twelve hours of sleep each night! He understands the necessity of sleep in bringing out full athletic potential. Most people don't have this much time to devote to sleep, but it proves the point.

We see the blessing of rest in God's Word. "By the seventh day God completed His work which He had done, and He RESTED on the seventh day from all His work which He had done. Then God blessed the seventh day and sanctified it, because in it He RESTED from all His work which God had created and made."—Genesis 2:2–3.

The Lord blessed the day that He rested and made it a holy day. God wants us to be able to rest in Him and His promises. Psalm 127 says, "He gives to His beloved even in his sleep." When you are in covenant with God, you can rest peacefully regardless of whatever situations are currently facing you. His peace will rest upon you, and you will wake up with newfound strength.

Even among a busy schedule, Jesus still found time to rest. He rested on a boat with His disciples and was fast asleep in the midst of a storm. When the disciples awoke Him out of fear for perishing, "He got up and rebuked the wind and said to the sea, "'Hush be still.' And the wind died down and it became perfectly calm."—Mark 4:39.

There are many people who have trouble going to sleep. No matter what the cause of this is in the natural, you can find abundance of rest in Jesus. Even when storms are around you, you can be sleeping peacefully as Jesus was because you have faith in your covenant with God.

Pray over your sleep. Declare you are the favored of the Lord and that He gives to you even in your sleep. Declare that in Jesus your yoke is easy and your burden is light according to Matthew 11:30. Whatever obstacle is stopping you from sleeping, command that mountain to be removed and cast into the sea (see Mark 11:23).

After the disciples had returned from being sent out on a mission by Jesus, he told them to "Come away by yourselves to a secluded place and rest a while." — Mark 6:31. Rest helps us not to burn out. It's a blessing from God and something that we shouldn't ignore. It is essential for regulating the functions of your physical body. It aids in muscle growth, regulating your metabolism, regulating your hormones, repairing your body, and renewing you with energy.

The Principle of Individualization

While these fitness principles are all true, everyone's body is different. What works for someone else to get in shape may not work the best for you. These fitness principles can help guide you in experimenting with differences in length, type, and intensity of your workouts. You can then find the workout plan that maximizes your health benefit.

Some people swear by one workout plan that "It's the best." In many cases, these people tried many different workout methods, but simply found what worked for them. It's not necessarily "the best," it's just the best workout for their body type. This is not an excuse to compromise with your workouts, but rather to find out how to maximize it.

Not only are people's physical bodies different, but their gifts in Christ are also different. 1 Corinthians 12 describes the body of Christ and how we are "individually members of it." No matter what part of the body you are (a foot, nose, eye, or hand), you are important to the overall function of the body.

"And He gave some as apostles, and some as prophets, and some as evangelists, and some as pastors and teachers, for the equipping of the saints for the work of service, to the building up of the body of Christ; until we all attain to the unity of the faith, and of the knowledge of the Son of God, to a mature man, to the measure of the stature which belongs to the fullness of Christ."—Ephesians 4:11–13. You may be different from someone else, but you are very important as an individual to the building up of the body of Christ!

THE PRINCIPLE OF CONSISTENCY/REVERSIBILITY

My brother Dave can throw a football with the best. Growing up, he always excelled at the position of quarterback. Throwing a perfect pass in a game wasn't a freak accident. Dave put in hours of practice each day. On our own, I'm sure that we have thrown over a million passes to each other!

Whether you're looking for a change in body composition or looking to maximize a component of physical fitness, you have to be consistent! Working out once a week is not going to change your body! Nor is working out hard for two weeks and then taking two months off. To get results, you need to stay to your workout and nutrition plan.

So many people fail to see results because they give up too early. The book of Galatians tells us, "In due time we will reap if we do not grow weary." Stay the course and pray for endurance. If you still don't see results, then try changing up your workout. Maybe it's time to increase the intensity or frequency of your workout.

Even if you achieve a certain level of physical fitness, it doesn't stay there automatically. While you don't have to work as hard to maintain this level as it took to get there, if you slack too much, you will begin to go backwards. This is the fitness principle of reversibility.

This principle is the same whether you are trying to maintain your body composition, speed, power, strength, or cardiovascular endurance. Your health and fitness isn't something to think about a few times a year or only for a season. It's part of living a healthy lifestyle where you are able to accomplish all of the tasks and assignments that God has for you.

The same principle is true in your relationship with God. Spending time with God is something that must be consistent. How can you grow in your walk without spending time with Him? How can you expect to hear the voice of God without taking time to listen? You have the AMAZING blessing of talking to the Almighty! The One true God! The Creator, Savior, Redeemer, King of kings, Lord of lords, Beginning and End, Provider, Healer, and God who LOVES you! The God who gave His only Son for you!

And yet, it is easy to put God on the backburner and spend time on other things. America has become hooked on entertainment. What if we spent the same amount of time with God that we spend on social media? What would our walk look like if we prayed as much as the TV was on?

1 Thessalonians 5:17 tells us to "pray without ceasing." This verse isn't telling you to sit on your knees and never move your whole life. It's telling you that your relationship with God should be constant. Praying to God is talking to God. You should be talking to Him without ceasing. God wants to be included in every aspect of your day. Every step and move you make should be in accordance with His will for you.

When you don't spend time with God, then your relationship with Him may begin to backslide, just like the principle of reversibility. YIKES! God doesn't want you to remain an infant in Christ, but wants you to become a mature man or woman of God. He wants you to step into the fullness of what He has for you. Don't turn from hot to lukewarm as a Christian. Keep pursuing, seeking, and loving.

THE PRINCIPLE OF SPECIFICITY

Your workout should be tailored to individually meet your needs. Not only does this vary depending upon your body type, but also on what your desired training outcome is. If you want to build speed, then you have to train for speed. If you want to build muscular strength, then you train for muscular strength. If you are training for a marathon, than you want to start running long distances. While there may be some crossover, your body responds specifically to the type of training you are performing. This is known as the principle of specificity.

For example, if you're a coach of a football team, you don't maximize the training of your team by having them run 6 miles every day. While this would help with the players' cardiovascular endurance, it would be training them for aerobic exercise and not anaerobic. Football is an anaerobic activity. It's a sport where players conduct short intense bursts of exercise followed by short periods of rest. To better condition his athletes, the coach should have them run sprints, hills, and short/intense activities. The athletes will build a better response to anaerobic exercise this way.

If you're trying to increase your muscular strength, then cross-country is not the best choice. While cross-country is fantastic for maximizing your cardiovascular endurance for aerobic exercises, it will not maximize your muscular strength. Olympic marathon runners will not bench press more than a professional football player. Nor will a professional football player have the muscular or cardiovascular endurance of an Olympic marathon runner.

God has designed your body to adapt based upon the stress put upon it. The type of change depends upon the type of stress. For example, let's look at muscle fibers in your legs. Your body is composed of two different types of muscle fiber (Type I and Type II: see the vocab section at the end of chapter 6 on muscle fibers).

You are born with a certain percentage of each fiber, but research has suggested that training can convert fibers from one type to the other. Or perhaps the training is influencing which muscle fiber type your body builds. If you broke down the fibers in an athlete's body, you would find that they have a high percentage of the muscle fiber type that is tailored to the sport they play. If you look at a professional athlete, these numbers are staggering, with the athlete being composed of 80 percent of the type of muscle fiber suited to their activity.

If you want the type of muscle that is suited for strength, then you tailor your workouts to build that fiber type by using heavy weight with smaller repetitions. If you want muscular endurance, then your workouts consist of high repetitions with lower weight.

Cross training has become very popular among many athletes. In this type of training, you constantly change your workout and focus on all areas of physical fitness. This is a great way to become very good at different types of physical activity and become a well-rounded athlete. Any type of physical activity you do is going to help you live a healthier lifestyle. However, if you want to maximize your performance in a particular area, then you would specifically focus on that area.

The principle of specificity is not accurate for your spiritual walk like the other principles are. Rather than counterbalancing each other, anything you do to further your relationship with God will increase it. It's important to not only get in the Word but to pray, to praise, to listen, to do good works, and to apply your faith. Everything is important and there is carryover by any of these areas to the other areas of your walk for God.

Now if you're lacking in a specific area, then obviously the principle of specificity would apply to increase that area by doing it more often. However, your level with God does not have to be a normal progression. He can accelerate you, give you revelation, wisdom, and understanding in a second that others have not achieved in a lifetime.

1 Corinthians 2: 10 states, "For to us God revealed them through the Spirit; for the Spirit searches all things, even the depths of God." When you accept Jesus into your heart, then the same spirit that raised Jesus Christ from the dead dwells in you! "Now we have received, not

the spirit of the world, but the Spirit who is from God, so that we may KNOW the things freely given to us by God."—1 Corinthians 2:12.

God's Spirit in us can reveal all things to us. It "teaches us all things," brings "to remembrance all that Jesus said," and gives us the "mind of Christ." Your past has no future. It doesn't matter at what age or time in your life you accepted Jesus as your Savior. He can accelerate you and use you RIGHT NOW! You don't have to wait. Step out in faith and watch how God will bring out your gifts and talents.

The Principle of Warming Up/Stretching

Warming up is an essential part of any workout or athletic event. Warming up helps prevent injury and allows your body to perform at optimal performance. As you move your body around and expend energy, your body will heat or "warm up." Your muscles respond and contract faster at this higher temperature.

When your body is in a relaxed state, only 15–20 percent of your blood flow goes to your muscles. After a few minutes of warming up, this blood flow increases to 70–75 percent (active.com 2014). This increased blood flow to your muscles leads to improved performance. The blood is carrying the oxygen and nutrients your muscles need!

So optimal performance occurs when the blood flow increases in your body…. Think about that statement for a second. The same principle is very true in relationship to the blood of Jesus. Optimal performance in life begins when you allow the blood of Jesus to wash you from all of your sins.

The blood of Jesus is what sanctifies you, makes you righteous, and gives you victory. You can't live out what God has for you if you aren't accepting what His Son did for you. What Jesus did is sufficient for you to have victory in every area of your life! However, that blood is only applied to your life when you let it.

"And they overcame him because of the blood of the Lamb and because of the word of their testimony, and they did not love their life even when faced with death."—Revelations 12:11. If you want to perform at optimal performance with your walk with God, and start overcoming, then let the blood of Jesus start flowing in your life!

Stretching is another foundation for most workout programs. Stretching can increase flexibility, prevent injury, and help you warm up. There are a few different types of stretching. **Dynamic stretching** is any type of stretch that involves movement. An example of this would be plyometrics, jumping jacks, or arm circles. Dynamic stretches are great for warming up your body and preparing it for either static stretches or exercise.

Static stretching is a fixed type of stretching with little movement. Examples of static stretching are touching your toes, stretching your arms above your head, or sticking out one leg in front of you for a calf stretch. Static stretches are great for increasing flexibility. They are best utilized at the end of a workout (to increase flexibility) or following a dynamic stretch or some other type of warm up. If you perform static stretches before your body is warmed up, then you can actually injure yourself.

Hundreds of athletes have pulled muscles stretching when stretching is supposed to be a preventative measure! Take a warm up lap, do some light jumping jacks, get the blood flowing, and then you can perform static stretches.

Ballistic stretching is a type of rhythmic stretching where you bounce back and forth in an attempt to increase your range of motion. Or, it is used in an eccentric contraction followed by a concentric contraction. For example, squatting down (eccentric) followed by an immediate jump (concentric) during a standing long jump or vertical leap. This type of stretching is ONLY used by experienced athletes seeking performance. It can easily lead to injury if done incorrectly. When mastered, this technique can be used to invoke the "stretch-shortening cycle" and produce greater force production.

PNF (Proprioceptive neuromuscular facilitation) stretching is a great technique to increase your range of motion. In this method of stretching, you both stretch and contract the targeted muscle group.

Take the standing quadriceps stretch, for example. To utilize the PNF technique, start with the normal stretch (grasping your foot with one of your hands and raising your leg behind you with the knee bent). Once you feel the stretch, try pushing down with your leg while using your hand/arm to resist and prevent movement. You are contracting the muscle while preventing the leg from moving. This is a form of the manual resistance technique. After you resist yourself for a few seconds, try doing the normal stretch again and see if you can stretch farther now. You will have likely increased the range of motion.

By increasing your flexibility, your muscles and joints will have a greater range of motion. Your muscles won't tear as easily and you will be able to bend/stretch to meet greater demands than before. You have to move into a position that is out of your comfort zone to perform a stretch. If you don't, then your flexibility will remain constant.

The same principle is true with your walk with God. If you only stay where you're comfortable and don't step out in faith, then you aren't going to experience growth. You need to stretch and push yourself to become more and more like Christ. When a challenge comes your way, it's not time to GET ready, it's time to BE ready. You should already be prepared to step out in faith and walk according to the Word rather than according to what you see.

THE PRINCIPLE OF HYDRATION

Your body is made up of an extremely high percentage of water. Water is essential for everyday function and to function at your optimal performance. If you don't keep yourself hydrated, then you will become tired, your body won't perform well, and you won't think as clearly. Hydration is a key whether you are trying to build muscle or trying to lose weight.

For those trying to build muscle, water will aid you in having the ability to complete a full workout. While the water itself isn't giving you the energy, it is the critical ingredient in allowing your body to utilize the energy it has.

Water will also aid in the process of absorbing nutrients like protein during the digestion process. It doesn't matter how much protein you intake if it isn't shipped to your muscles! Did you know that there is water in your cells? If a muscle cell is short on water, then that cell can actually shrink in size. We want muscle cells to become bigger, so we need to keep them fed with an adequate supply of water!

Sometimes when people think they are hungry they are really just thirsty! Instead of consuming lots of food and feeling like you need more, you could have just had a drink of water! Water will help calm your appetite. If you're struggling just to make it to lunch, then you are probably dehydrated. Your body can survive for over a month without food but only a few days without water! Hmmm, maybe water is important?

Not only do we thirst in the natural, but people thirst spiritually as well. There is only one source of life that will truly fulfill this thirst, and that source is Jesus. People can tell when there is a void in their life. Instead of turning to God, people try to fill this void with sex, drugs, adrenaline, or immorality.

While these things may seem to gratify a temporary desire, they will never truly satisfy the individual. The individual will "thirst" again and will continue in a downward spiral to quench this desire. Sin separates you from God. What may have tasted like honey at first will become bitter. "Then when lust has conceived, it gives birth to sin; and when sin is accomplished, it brings forth death." —James 1:15.

Run to the true source of life! Jesus tells the woman at the well, "If you knew the gift of God, and who it is who says to you, 'Give Me a drink,' you would have asked Him, and He would have given you living water." —John 4:10. He then tells her, "Everyone who drinks of this water shall thirst again; but whoever drinks of the water that I shall give him shall never thirst; but the water that I shall give him shall become in him a well of water springing up to eternal life." —John 4:13.

Now that you have been filled with the true source of life, you can pour out that life to others. "Jesus stood and cried out, saying, 'If anyone is thirsty, let him come to Me and drink. He who believes in Me, as the Scripture said, "From his innermost being will flow rivers of living water."'" God has filled you with His Spirit and with power to be His witnesses throughout the earth and pour out living water!

We have gone through a bunch of fitness principles! As we discovered, many of these fitness principles line up with spiritual truths. Implement these principles to maximize the efficiency of your workouts and thus your reach out. Before we break down various workouts, we have an extremely important spiritual law to cover. I didn't include the law in this section because it deserves a whole chapter of its own.

Chapter 7

THE LAW OF
SOWING AND REAPING

The more active you are, the greater your health will be. The harder you work out, the stronger you get. The harder or longer you work out, the more calories you burn. The harder or longer your workout, the higher your metabolism will be. The greater the intensity is, the quicker/greater the impact will be. Whatever you put into your workout is what you get out of it. You REAP what you SOW!

This fitness principle is not just a principle, it's a spiritual law. This law relates to all of the other principles and has a huge impact on every area of your life. You can see the law of sowing and reaping throughout the Bible.

- "Do not be deceived, God is not mocked; for whatever a man sows, this he will also reap. For the one who sows to his own flesh will from the flesh reap corruption, but the one who sows to the Spirit will from the Spirit reap eternal life. Let us not lose heart in doing good, for in due time we will reap if we do not grow weary." — Galatians 6:7–9

- "Now this I say, he who sows sparingly will also reap sparingly, and he who sows bountifully will also reap bountifully." 2 Corinthians 9:6

- "Therefore, my beloved brethren, be steadfast, immovable, always abounding in the work of the Lord, knowing that your toil is not in vain in the Lord." 1 Corinthians 15:58

- "There is one who scatters, and yet increases all the more, And there is one who withholds what is justly due, and yet it results only in want. The generous man will be prosperous, And he who waters will himself be watered." Proverbs 11:24–25

- "He who is generous will be blessed, For he gives some of his food to the poor." Proverbs 22:9

- "According to what I have seen, those who plow iniquity and those who sow trouble harvest it."—Job 4:8

- "You have plowed wickedness, you have reaped injustice, You have eaten the fruit of lies. Because you have trusted in your way, in your numerous warriors"—Hosea 10:13

- "Death and life are in the power of the tongue, And those who love it will eat its fruit."—Proverbs 18:21

- "For by your words you will be justified, and by your words you will be condemned."—Matthew 12:37

- "Say to the righteous that it will go well with them, For they will eat the fruit of their actions" Isaiah 3:10

- "When you shall eat of the fruit of your hands, You will be happy and it will be well with you"—Psalm 128:2

- "Now it shall be, if you diligently obey the LORD your God, being careful to do all His commandments which I command you today, the LORD your God will set you high above all the nations of the earth."—Deut 28:1

- "But you shall serve the LORD your God, and He will bless your bread and your water; and I will remove sickness from your midst"—Exodus 23:25

- Check out Deuteronomy 28, the whole chapter shows the law of sowing and reaping.

Wow, that's a lot of different verses! But honestly that is only a small portion of the law of sowing and reaping shown throughout the Bible. There is a consequence to every action, deed, and word you say. There is also a consequence for every lack of action, deed, or word you say.

If you obey God's commandments, and live for Him, then you will be blessed! God has wonderful rewards for the righteous. The ultimate reward is eternal life through Jesus Christ our Lord!

However, don't miss out on all of the blessings that God has for you RIGHT NOW. These blessings aren't limited to heaven. Jesus said, "Repent, for the kingdom of heaven is at hand."—Matthew 4:17.

There is a new heaven and new earth that is coming, but Christ's reign has already started and is NOW. Many of the above blessings achieved through obedience were under the old covenant. How much more do we have those blessings and more under the new covenant in Jesus! God has given you the ability to reap blessings by sowing righteousness.

The law of sowing and reaping applies to your finances too (as many of the above verses show). God tells the Israelites in Malachi 3, "Will a man rob God? Yet you are robbing Me! But you say, 'How have we robbed you?' In tithes and offerings. You are cursed with a curse, for you are robbing Me, the whole nation of you! Bring the whole tithe into the storehouse, so that there may be food in My house, and test Me now in this," says the Lord of hosts, "if I will not open the windows of heaven and pour out for you a blessing until it overflows."—Malachi 3:8–10.

God wants you to trust Him in your finances and have faith in His covenant with you. Tithe is not an option but a commandment. When you don't tithe, you are reaping poverty. On the other hand when you sow, then God will open the windows of heaven for you.

On top of tithe, we are commanded to bring in offerings. Tithe is 10 percent of your income. Offerings are anything that you give on top of that. While tithe keeps you in covenant with God, offerings are the key to increasing your finances.

Paul tells us that your harvest will be according to your seed; that you reap either sparingly or bountifully depending upon whether you sowed sparingly or bountifully (see above verse 1 Corinthians 9:6). You can't outgive God. Jesus said, "Give, and it will be given to you. They will pour into your lap a good measure—pressed down, shaken together, and running over. For by your standard of measure it will be measured to you in return."—Luke 6:38.

I have watched God supernaturally bless my finances since I've become obedient to tithe and offerings.

You see the law of sowing and reaping in nutrition. If you put unhealthy things into your body, then your body will reap destruction. If you sow good nutrients into your body, then you will reap good health.

The law is in effect with what you say. Your words have power. If you speak faith and life, then you receive God's promises. If you speak doubt and unbelief, then you are missing out on God's promises for your life. If you have good friends around you, then you will be sharpened. If you surround yourself with bad company, then it can corrupt your morals.

You even see the law of sowing and reaping with music! Listen to bad music with bad lyrics and it will have a negative impact on you. Listen to lyrics that build you up and you will be encouraged. The law of sowing and reaping is everywhere.

If you walk by faith in God and follow His commandments, then you will have many blessings in your life and He will use you to glorify His name! "My Father is glorified by this, that you bear much fruit, and so prove to be My disciples."—John 15:8. God wants you to do good works as He did and He is glorified in the fruit you bear!

Now that we have seen that this spiritual law is very much in effect, let's break down how it specifically relates to physical fitness. Here are some of the things you will reap from increased physical activity in your life.

More Physical Activity =

- Increase in the health-related components of physical fitness (flexibility, muscular strength, muscular endurance, body composition, cardiovascular endurance)
- Depending upon type of activity, increase in skill-related components of physical fitness (power, speed, balance, coordination)
- Improved posture, balance, and mobility
- Decrease in stress level
- Increase in positive mood and attitude
- Decrease in cardiovascular disease, cancer, sickness, strokes, and type II diabetes
- Increase in body's immune system
- Increase in resting metabolic rate
- Decrease in body fat
- Increase of activities that you are now physically able to perform for Christ
- Increase of energy level that you have to do the works that God has called you to do
- Increased self-image and self-efficacy
- Increase in overall physical ability

The more you sow into your body with your workouts, the more you will reap these benefits. If you only workout once a week, then you aren't going to reap great results. The law of sowing and reaping is in effect during your workout as well. If you don't put forth much effort during a workout, then you are shortchanging your results. You should be exhausted after a workout, pushing yourself to your limits.

I remember how I felt after my first "three a day" workout during preseason of high school football. I had pushed myself harder than I ever had before, and that was the intent of the training. I was so sore the next day that I felt like I could barely walk (even though I was fine once I had warmed up properly). Over the next few weeks, my body adjusted to the new intensity and duration of our practices. By the time the season started, our team was in the best physical shape to date, which was the goal.

It was the same principle at basic training for the military. We sowed a lot of physical exercise, and we reaped results! One of my teammates started out running a twenty-four-minute two-mile run. By graduation, he was running the two miles in fifteen minutes and passed the test to graduate!

I remember how hard my first two-mile ruck march was at basic. But by continuing to sow hard work, most of our unit completed the 18-mile ruck march. Even before the military, I watched hard work pay off with exercise. In one year, I improved my pushup score from 30 pushups to 70, one pull-up to 7, and increased my sit-up score from 60 to 80. By continuing to sow, I can now do over 100 pushups in two minutes, 18 pull-ups, and over 100 sit-ups in two minutes.

The law of sowing and reaping is constantly going on in your life—whether it's with your walk with God, your finances, your words, your relationships, or your fitness. You reap what you sow. If you want to be physically fit, then it's time to sow by working out. And not just working out, but working out hard! Remember: if you sow sparingly you reap sparingly, but if you sow generously, then you reap generously.

Chapter 8

WORKOUTS TO REACH OUT

You may be wondering, *How do I apply all of this information? I'm ready to work out, but where do I start?* At this point you understand the importance of fitness to your walk as a Christian. You understand how your mind, words, and faith impact your ability to become physically fit. You understand the fitness and spiritual principles that will help you achieve your goal. Now it's time to get equipped with the right workout that is tailored for you!

The Workout to Lose Weight!

I'll start with this workout since it's probably the most popular. Currently in America, one third of all adults are labeled as obese. Two thirds of current adults are labeled as being overweight. How did this happen?

Perhaps the biggest culprit is America's food system. Most of our food is processed with added chemicals and preservatives. It's important to eat foods as close to their natural form as possible. Try to eat them in the condition that God made them.

Your body doesn't respond well to added chemicals. For some of these chemicals, your body actually surrounds them with fat! It doesn't recognize them and performs this as a protective measure rather than breaking the chemicals down.

Unhealthy food is very affordable. It's quick, easy, and cheap. It's loaded with unhealthy fats, sugar, excess calories, and harmful chemicals. Check out the nutrition section for how to eat healthy and feel great! Eating well is just as important as working out. They go hand in hand with each other, and you must do both to maximize results and truly see change in your body composition.

The other main culprit of obesity is a sedentary lifestyle. God designed your body to move! Movement requires energy above your resting metabolic rate (RMR). RMR is the amount of calories that you burn while your body is at rest. Movement causes your body to burn additional calories above this rate. These calories are essential to burn the calories you need to have a deficit in your caloric intake (the amount of calories you take in a day). Staying active is a primary key to losing or maintaining your weight.

Here is the obesity cycle of America. Many Americans realize they want to lose weight. Due to this, they go on a diet. Few Americans realize, however, that too strict of a diet can lower your metabolism. If your body doesn't get a certain amount of calories, it thinks its starving, and will burn muscle instead of burning fat!

Muscles are more metabolically active than fat. If you are losing muscle, you are losing one of the keys to having a higher RMR. Your RMR will also drop during a strict diet since your body goes into starvation mode and tries to conserve energy. So even if you have some success in your diet and lose ten pounds, you will have a harder time keeping it off. Most people gain this weight back, and then go on an even stricter diet!

This leads to some people eating salads for every meal and yet they can't drop a pound! *They seem to gain weight just by looking at food.* How do you beat this cycle? EXERCISE! Exercise will allow you to either maintain or raise your metabolism while you are on your diet. You will lose weight even faster and you can keep it off! It's the fastest way to lose weight and the way to maintain your new body composition.

It's okay to go on a diet if that means you are eating healthy foods and eating healthy proportions. Proper nutrition is just as important as exercise. However, don't go overboard to where you're NOT eating a healthy amount of calories in a day. Don't ever go below 1000 calories!

Eating too few calories prevents your body from burning mode. Eat the right food, in the right proportions, and you will find success. It's healthier to lose a few pounds each week than to try and lose it all in one day. Okay, so physical activity along with a proper diet is the way to lose weight! But what type of physical activity? How do you accelerate this process?

ACCELERATE YOUR WEIGHT LOSS

All exercises are good for you, but there are certain types of exercise that will accelerate your weight loss process. To do so, you need to maximize the calories burned during your workout and maximize the calories burned AFTER your workout.

The calories burned during your workout are in a direct relationship to the intensity and duration of your workout. You burn more calories when you work out at a higher intensity. It's the law of sowing and reaping again. The more energy and effort you sow, the more calories you burn.

Your metabolism rises above the RMR (resting metabolic rate) to meet the increased demand of energy. While calories burned during the workout are important, it's the calories burned afterward that are the key to accelerating your weight loss.

Continuing to burn calories following your workout has become known to the fitness community as the "afterburn effect." The afterburn effect is maximized in your body when you exercise at a high intensity. If you look at any great weight loss program, such as the *Biggest Loser*, P90X, CrossFit, or Insanity, you will notice that all of these programs are performed at a HIGH INTENSITY. The maximized afterburn effect in your body at a high intensity is due to the body's demand to return to a resting state. The energy demand to return to a resting state in your body is in a direct relationship to the intensity and duration of the exercise.

For example, if you perform exercise at a high intensity, you may find that your breathing rate is elevated for minutes after the exercise. Your body is continuing to take in oxygen in an effort to help your body recover. This process is known as EPOC (excess post exercise oxygen consumption). EPOC is one of the factors involved in the afterburn effect.

Your body also will have a raised metabolism following exercise, to clear out lactate from your body. Lactate accumulates rapidly when you work out at a high intensity. This is why many long-distance runners run at a pace right below their lactate threshold (aka second ventilatory threshold). By not maximizing their top speed, the runner accumulates less lactate, and can run for a longer period of time. But by working out at a high intensity, your body will have an increased workload to clear out the lactate following exercise. This workload is another part of the afterburn effect.

The rebuilding process in your body is another part of the afterburn effect. It takes energy to rebuild the ATP-PCr energy system. It also takes energy to rebuild broken down muscle (one of the reasons strength training is great for the afterburn effect).

Besides helping with the afterburn effect, strength training is valuable to increase your RMR (resting metabolic rate). Muscle is more metabolically active than fat. The greater the percentage of fat-free mass in your body, the higher your RMR will be. So not only will strength training help you maximize the afterburn effect, but it will also increase the percentage of fat-free mass in your body, which will in turn help you burn even more calories! Your RMR "accounts for about 60 percent to 75 percent of the total energy we expend each day" (Wilmore, 499). Even a small increase in RMR can equate to thousands of calories burned each year.

With the afterburn effect, you are still burning additional calories above your RMR hours later while you're on the couch. With a raised RMR due to a higher percentage of fat-free mass, you are also burning additional calories. High intensity workouts, especially those that occasionally involve strength training, are a recipe for success to lose weight.

I'm not saying that you can't go jogging to workout. There is nothing wrong with a low-intensity exercise such as jogging. It's a great activity for building cardiovascular endurance and muscular endurance in your legs. Coupled with high intensity training, it can help burn fat and maximize weight loss. One of my clients averaged a weight loss of 4 pounds a week by coupling these two together. However, performing **only** low intensity exercises will NOT accelerate your weight loss! You are missing out on burning extra calories.

If you are going to run, try sets of sprints at a high intensity instead of jogging. There are also forms of cardio that incorporate a resistance element. Swimming is a great full body exercise that is strenuous on both your heart and your muscles. Or try a program like Crossfit that is so fast-paced that you work on cardio the same time that you are working on strength training.

Another great way to keep your metabolism charged is to perform what I call "bursts" throughout the day. Bursts are three minutes of intense physical exercise. For example, performing a set of burpees for three minutes.

Let's say that you perform five 3-minute bursts a day on top of your 45-minute workout. That's only an additional 15 minutes of exercise a day. However, since your bursts are throughout the day, they help keep your body in "burning mode." Your body will continue to burn and this will in turn maximize the afterburn effect. This may be a lot of new information, so here is a summarized list of the keys to accelerate your weight loss.

WEIGHT LOSS TIPS

1. Pray over your workouts and put God first in them. (This is the most important step. Let God give you wisdom on what is the perfect workout and nutrition plan for you.)
2. Work out five to six times a week. Build up to this if you have to (start at three times a week). Try to work out for 60 minutes or do two different 30-minute sessions at different times in the day.
3. Stay consistent; find a way to squeeze workouts into your day. Anything is better than nothing.
4. Incorporate some form of strength training into at least half of your workouts. (This builds muscle, which raises your RMR since muscle is more metabolically active than fat.)
5. Workout out at high intensity! This maximizes the calories that you will burn DURING and AFTER your workout (due to EPOC, removal of lactate, and rebuilding of energy systems/ muscles).
6. Eat healthy! Don't negate all of your hard work. Eating healthy is just as important as working out. Eat whole foods, avoid sweets, use proper proportions, and don't go on a crazy strict diet! Eat five to six meals a day.
7. Get 7–9 hours of sleep each day
8. Hydrate yourself with lots of water!
9. Perform five three-minute bursts throughout your day.

Chapter 9

STRENGTH TRAINING WORKOUTS

P roverbs 20:29 tells us, "The glory of young men is their strength." During our graduation ruck march of basic training, I was able to take some of my teammate's weight load and carry it on top of my own. My teammate was struggling during the march, and soldiers always help a battle buddy out. I've helped a lot of people move out of their old house and into a new one. Carrying couches, as simple as that task may sound, can really help to bless someone. I love seeing the grateful smiles on their faces.

I praise God for the strength to accomplish physical tasks like this. I'm thankful for the ones I could perform, and the tasks that I couldn't perform push me to become stronger. I've had times where I've succeeded and times where I have failed. Failure is only failure if you accept it. God has called you to be healthy and strong, and strength training is one of the best ways to achieve this.

Strength training is a great form of exercise. It increases muscular hypertrophy (muscle size), the strength of your muscles, the percentage of Type II muscle fibers, can help with the afterburn effect, and can increase all of the health-related components of physical fitness. Wow, that's a lot! Strength training may not increase your cardiovascular endurance as much as some activities (such as intense running, biking, or swimming), but it can still benefit this component if performed at a fast pace.

So what fundamentals do you need to know before including strength training in your exercise routine? Here are some fundamentals of strength training that you need to maximize effectiveness and prevent injury.

Full Range of Motion

Exercising through a full range of motion is very important. If you don't do this, then you are only strengthening part of the muscle you are working on. To strengthen the full muscle, you need to allow all of the different muscle fibers to shorten and lengthen. This shortening (concentric contraction) and lengthening (eccentric contraction) process is necessary to fully break down muscle fibers.

Isolate the Muscle/Proper Form

Have you ever seen someone, while in a gym, using the whole body to lift a weight that is designed to be lifted by only one muscle? Someone who is more focused on impressing those around than on getting stronger? Someone who is trying to lift more weight he or she can handle, and due to this, is using improper form? I think we all have. If you want to get stronger, then don't focus on those around you. Remember your body is the Lord's; you should be lifting for Him and not for others.

To strengthen a muscle, you need to isolate it during the exercise. This means that if you're trying to improve the strength of your bicep that you only use your bicep to lift the weight. Or if you're focusing on your chest, then you use your chest to lift the weight. While other muscles may help some in the performance of the exercise, you want to isolate the intended muscle as much as possible.

If you are swinging your whole body around to lift a weight, then you are using momentum and not your muscle fibers. This means that you are not putting stress on your fibers and they are not being broken down! When you lift, use a weight that you can lift with proper form. If you can't do this, then lower the weight. Practice doesn't make perfect. Perfect practice makes perfect. Bad practice produces minor results.

I see this same principle at work with my experience in the military. We train the way we plan to fight. If my infantry unit trained just to look cool and didn't apply real tactics, then we would be preparing to fail. Looking cool doesn't help when people are trying to kill you. While in Iraq, we conducted many different missions. All of these missions relied on the basics that we rehearsed over and over. Don't worry about others in the gym. Have perfect practice, perfect reps, and maximize the energy you are sowing into your workout.

Now there are some exercises that utilize the whole body. While you are using many different muscle groups to perform these exercises, they still need to be performed properly. Improper form will put stress on your joints and bones rather than your muscles. To maximize muscular growth, you have to maximize the tension put on your fibers, and that requires proper form.

Controlled Movement

When lifting weights, it is essential to control the movement. This is especially true for beginners. If you are lifting and dropping the weight too fast, then you have an increased chance for injury. It's much better to have a slow and smooth motion when you lift.

When you become more experienced, then you can add some speed to certain phases of the lift depending on what results you want. For example, many athletes perform the concentric phase (the shortening phase of the motion) very fast to build explosion. This is the phase of the lift where you are going against gravity and is often referred to as the "positive" phase. For example, pushing up very fast from a squat on the positive phase would be a way to build explosion or power in your legs.

On the other hand, there can be benefits to slowing down the exercise. One of the best ways to build strength is to have a slow lowering phase (negative or eccentric contraction). This aids in putting ultimate tension on your muscle fibers and forcing them to recruit muscle fibers that they wouldn't have needed if the repetition was performed at a high speed.

No matter what speed you are performing the exercise at, you must make sure you are in control. If you're just starting, lift the positive phase on a two-second count and the negative phase on a four-second count. This is a solid method to begin with. Speed can build power, but slow negative phases can help maximize strength gains. With any exercise program, individuals are different (see Principle of Individuality), and you need to find what works for you.

REPETITIONS AND WEIGHT

Strength training is a great way to increase both muscular strength and muscular endurance. Depending upon the weight and repetitions you are using, you may be tailoring towards one component or the other. In review, muscular strength is the MAX FORCE you can apply for one repetition. Muscular endurance is HOW LONG you can continually perform the exercise with your muscles before failure. Muscular strength can be tested by your max bench press, while muscular endurance would be tested by a benching a lower weight (60 percent max) and seeing how many repetitions you could perform before failure.

During basic training, the army focuses heavily upon building muscular endurance. New soldiers have not earned the luxury of going to a weight room. Instead, these green recruits are pummeled with body weight exercises constantly by drill sergeants. As training progresses, soldiers find that their muscular endurance is increasing. They are able to do more and more repetitions before failure.

The soldiers' muscular strength will also increase in the beginning. However, once they are accustomed to their body weight, it will begin to plateau. To truly increase muscular strength, these soldiers will have to either do an insane amount of body weight exercises (more than their muscles have become accustomed to) or increase the weight. They have to find a way to put max tension on their muscle fibers. Soldiers could increase the weight by adding on weight to their body (like a loaded combat vest), adding manual resistance, or by going to a gym. If you want to increase your muscular strength, you have to gradually add weight.

For example, let's say you can bench press 135 pounds six times. After working out for three weeks, you can now perform twelve repetitions using the same weight instead of six. Now would be a good time to increase the weight to 140 or 145 pounds. Once you increase the weight, your repetitions may decrease to around six again. After a couple of weeks, you can do twelve repetitions again, and the process repeats as you add more weight. Increasing your muscular strength can help your muscular endurance jump up to a new level. Since your max is higher, you may find that you can perform an amazing amount of reps at your starting weight.

When you work out, you should strive to perform either more repetitions than before or perform the repetitions at a higher weight. By continuing to increase and following the principle of overload (see Principle of Overload), your muscles will have to grow to meet the new challenge. Tearing down muscle fibers requires tension and a strain to be put on them. This is not accomplished by lifting what you are accustomed to.

So what's the perfect number of repetitions to build strength? Or what's the perfect number to build endurance? This is a much debated question and it really depends on what works for you. You have to find what puts the most strain on your muscles. However, for most people, lifting heavy weights with low reps tailors towards strength, while lots of repetitions tailors more to endurance.

Alternating the two has also been proven to work for some people to maximize their strength and prevent plateauing. Here is a modified chart to help guide you based off the one found in the *ACE Personal Trainer Manual* taken from the *Essentials of Strength Training and Conditioning* by Champaign.

Training Goal	Sets	Repetitions	Weight
General muscle fitness	1–2	8–15	60–80 percent max
Muscular endurance	2–3	≥ 12	60–70 percent max
Muscular strength	2–6	≤ 6	80–90 percent max
Muscular hypertrophy (muscle size)	3–6	6–12	70–80 percent max
Power, Single effort events Multiple-effort events	3–5 3–6	1–2 3–5	Moderate weight with fast movement

The key is finding ways to continue to overload your muscle fibers and force them to grow. In the next section, I'm going to provide you with several different approaches for strength training. It's up to you to find the method that works best for you (see Principle of Individualization). The best way to accomplish this is through prayer. Ask God to give you wisdom on how to best take care of your body. Then work out hard and observe the results. You should stay with a training method long enough to see if it is really working or not. Start with the recommendations from the chart. If you aren't getting the results you are looking for, then try a different method.

Rest/Frequency of workouts

What about the amount of rest in-between sets? How much rest do you need in-between workouts? This area is thoroughly covered under the Rest Principle section in Chapter 6. However, here is the basic table from that chapter, to give you a reminder of the general recommendations based upon the *ACE Personal Trainer manual.*

Activity	Rest Intervals during Workout	Amount of Rest after workout
Aerobic low intensity cardio	≥ 20 minutes	24 hours
Anaerobic high intensity	≤ 5 minutes	24–48 hours
Muscular strength	2–5 minutes	72 hours
Muscular endurance	1–2 minutes ≤30–60 seconds high intensity	48 hours
Muscular hypertrophy	30–90 seconds	48 hours–72 hours
Power	2–5 minutes	48–72 hours

STRENGTH TRAINING APPROACHES:

Upper and Lower Split

This approach is characterized by alternating upper body and lower body workouts. For example, working out upper body on Monday, lower body on Tuesday, and then repeating until a rest day. A pro to this approach is that muscles will have 48 hours to recover (and even more if you have a rest day twice or once a week). Adding a different workout on a third day (like cardio) would give you the 72 hours required for recovery from workouts tailored towards muscular strength.

Another benefit to this approach is simplicity. Rather than worry about which muscles to lift, you simply lift either your arms or legs/ abs. If you wanted to add variety into this routine, you could combine a split set approach with a cardio/running/ or abdominal day. For example, upper body on Monday, lower body on Tuesday, Variety day on Wednesday. You could then repeat the routine and then Sunday off.

Due to lifting a lot of different muscles on lifting days, this approach would also release a lot of hormones that aid in muscular growth (although not as much as the next approach).

Full Body Workout Approach

In this approach, you always conduct full body workouts. A full body workout is a workout that involves all of the major muscle groups in your body. Some athletes believe that full body workouts release the most hormones due to lifting many different muscle groups. These hormones are thought to help produce more muscular hypertrophy than normal workouts.

A con to this approach, however, is the threat of over- or under-training. If you perform full body workouts every day, one might question whether or not your body has had time to fully recover. And if you have an off day in-between, then you are only working out three to four times a week. Of course, this could be corrected by adding a cardio or aerobic form of training on the off days to add more volume to your training regimen. You could also have "lighter" and "heavier" days but lift the same muscles.

Remember that people differ in their recovery times needed for muscular growth. There are athletes who can use the same muscles groups every day and still increase. For others, this approach would contradict itself and inhibit muscular growth. Once again, it's important to see how your body responds and pray for direction in your workout routine.

If you start to plateau on a certain muscle group, then you aren't overloading enough. Keep your normal workout routine, but start exhausting this muscle group three out of four days on top of that to break through the plateau. Continue to do this for a week or two and you should break through the plateau. If this doesn't work, then try the opposite approach and add more rest days for that muscle group.

Muscle Isolation approach

Another philosophy on strength training is to isolate only a few muscles on each lifting day. For example: Monday = biceps/triceps, Tuesday = chest/shoulders, Wednesday = legs, Thursday = back/neck/abdominals, Friday= sprint workout. By isolating only a few muscle groups, it's easier to fully exhaust them. You can do multiple sets to failure and have a high volume of repetitions.

This approach is very effective at putting an intense strain and tension on your muscle fibers. Another benefit to this approach is that your muscles will have time to recover since you don't work out the same muscles every day.

This approach is my personal favorite. I seem to get the best results with a variation of this workout style—for example, lifting chest/back/shoulders on Monday, biceps and triceps on Tuesday, legs, abs, and sprints on Wednesday. I repeat for the next three days but target the muscles slightly different. I then rest on Sunday. This is a mix of an upper/lower split and the muscle isolation approach. It gives each muscle group 72 hours to recover, breaks down muscle fibers fully, and allows for two workouts of each body part each week.

Muscle confusion Approach

Similar to the muscle isolation approach is the idea of muscle confusion. In this philosophy, you do a different workout every day. You may repeat workouts once every two weeks. By constantly changing the demands on your muscles, they have to constantly adapt. This approach is recommended to prevent plateauing. It allows ample time for muscle recovery and helps the user not get bored of the same routine. This approach is used by CrossFit.

Are you ready to hit the gym and crush some weights? You now know the fundamentals and approaches necessary to increase your strength. Remember that you can do nothing apart from God, but all things through Him. Your strength training should be part of your overall goal to take care of the body God has given you and maximize what He has called you to do. Working out to reach out. Your strength is in God. Ephesians 6:10 tells us, "Be strong in the Lord and in the strength of His might."

Chapter 10

HOME WORKOUTS

Your kids sprint up to greet you with big smiles as you open the door to your happy home. "Can we play with you before dinner? What are we doing tonight?" Your thoughts of going to the gym today fly out the window. You know that this time with your family is more important.

What if you don't have time to go to the gym? Or what if you're a parent and don't want to leave your kids at home while you go workout? Don't worry—there are plenty of ways to work out right inside your own home! The only excuse you have is the one you make. Find a way to consistently exercise!

If the weather is nice, you can always workout outside. Whether it's a running workout, playing sports, or a fun physical activity like hiking, there are plenty of ways to get moving! There are also numerous ways to work out while staying inside your own home. For most of these exercises, you don't need ANY equipment!

However, let me first offer some suggestions on household items that can be converted into exercise equipment. I will then break down the different exercises.

Homemade Exercise Equipment

- **Chairs**: Chairs can be a great tool for creating exercises. Turn two chairs to face opposite each other with their backs facing in. Stand in between the two chairs and now you have your own dip bar! Use your hands to spring up and curl your feet so they don't hit the ground while you perform your dips. A dip is where you lower and raise your body using only your arms. Dips are a great exercise to improve your triceps muscle.
  - o If the chairs move too much, place something heavy on each of them to keep them in place. You can also sit in the chair and use it to aid your back in an exercise such as "seated press." However, make sure the chair is sturdy and stable enough before trying this.
  - o A chair can also be used to perform negative dips. Place your hands on the end of the chair and walk your feet out. Then lower and raise your body using your arms.
  - o If you have a supportive chair, you may sit in it and utilize it for seated press or military press (raising weights above your shoulder and back down).
- **Weights**: You can utilize almost anything in your house and turn it into a weight. Try to find a heavy object that you can grip easily and safely. This object can then be used for exercises such as bicep curls, triceps extensions, and shoulder press.
  - o Water weighs 8 pounds per gallon. Any gallon of liquid that you have in your fridge (for example a gallon of milk) can be utilized as a weight. Most of these gallons come with a handle which allows you to have a safe and functional grip for the weight. Even if a gallon of milk is the heaviest object you can find, it's still better than not having a weight at all.
  - o During basic training in the Army, I was introduced to "Rifle PT." It's physical training using the very rifle that

you carry. While the rifle doesn't weigh much, it starts to feel that way after dozens of repetitions! The training helped make us accustomed to the weight of the rifle and allowed us to carry and shoot it with ease.

- **Backpack**: I have found a backpack to be one of the most effective homemade weights. Load up a backpack with textbooks or any other heavy item. You can then weigh the backpack on the scale to get an exact weight.
  - o Backpacks come with handles and straps. Both can be used to allow you to have a safe and functional grip. Backpacks are perfect for many upper body exercises (such as bicep curls). You can also wear the backpack to give yourself added resistance during exercise (such as pull ups or dips).
- **Pull up bars**: You can buy a pull up bar for your house for about twenty dollars. They make bars that fit in your doorway and can be put up and taken down easily. If you don't want to spend the money, try walking outside and look to see if there is a nearby tree. Low and sturdy branches are great pull up bars. If you live near a playground, you can use the monkey bars or the top of a swing as your pull up bar.
- **Resistance bands**: Resistance bands are a low-cost item and use very little space in your house. These bands come in different sizes to allow you to pick the specific amount of resistance that you want. They can be used to add resistance in a variety of exercises.
- **Wall**: Try climbing your legs up a nearby wall. This can help with decline pushups or even shoulder press if you climb your legs up high enough. If you turn around so that you are facing the wall, try walking your legs up it. Once they are midway up the wall, there are multiple lifts you can do with your butt or abdominal muscles. Your hands should be palms down on

the ground at your sides to give you the support to try various motions from this position.

- **Couch**: Many couches have a space underneath that you can fit your feet under. Since the couch is heavy, it is now the perfect spotter for your sit-ups!

- **Manual resistance**: Manuel resistance is a great technique to build strength that utilizes zero equipment! All you need is another person to work out with. The other person applies pressure opposite of the direction you are lifting. By controlling the amount of pressure, the spotter tailors the amount of resistance on the lifter. For example, the spotter could press down on the back of the lifter to make pushups more difficult.

HOME EXERCISES

UPPER BODY EXERCISES

- **Pushups**: A great upper body exercise! This exercise can be used as a substitute for bench press. It is a staple of military training and many strength programs. Pushups work primarily on building your chest but they also work your back and triceps.
  - From a kneeling position, lean forward and place your hands on the floor beneath your shoulders. Stretch out your legs behind you so that you're balancing on your toes and your hands. Your body should be in a general straight line. This position is known as the "Front Leaning Rest" position. A common mistake is to sag your body in the middle or to lift your butt high in the air.
  - While remaining straight, lower your body until your arms are at a 90 degree angle (your chest should be almost touching the ground at this point). Extend your

arms back up to the starting position and then repeat. Make sure you extend all the way back up to the starting position. "Cheater pushups" won't give you the full range of motion necessary to work the complete muscle.

o To work different muscle groups, try doing a variety of different types of pushups. Spread your arms out wide or make a diamond with your hands and do close grip pushups. Try pushups using only your fingertips, using only one arm, or lifting one of your legs up in the air.

o Lift either your legs or hands up onto another surface (like a chair) to perform incline or decline pushups. This variation will allow you to work muscle groups you may have missed in your home workout routine. It also allows for one of your muscle groups to recover while you perform additional repetitions.

- **Dips**: Dips are a fantastic exercise to build your triceps. Remember that chairs are a great tool to make your own dip bar. All you need is two .parallel surfaces.  Lift yourself off the ground with a hand balanced on either chair/ surface. Curl your feet (so they don't hit the floor) and lower yourself until your arms are at (or just below) a 90 degree angle. Extend your arms back up to the starting position.

o The straighter your back, the more this exercise focuses on your triceps muscle. The more you lean forward, the more the dip will be spread out on your chest. Can't do a regular dip? That's okay! There are other exercises you can do to work up to it.

o Bench dips are a great way to build up your triceps and most people can perform them. Find a bench (or use a chair again) and place your hands on its edge. Walk your legs far out in front of you so that you are supporting your body weight with your hands. Lower yourself to the ground (arms near a 90 degree angle) and then use your arms to press back up. They might not hurt much at first but do them for a minute and your triceps will be pulsing! Negative dips is another common name for this exercise.

- **Pull ups/chin ups**: Pull ups are a fantastic upper body exercise! The amount of different muscle groups they can work is astounding. Pull ups can work your biceps, triceps, trapezius, chest, back, lats, abs, and obliques! Find a bar, a tree branch, or anything you can grab safely. Use your upper body to raise your chin up above the bar and then lower yourself back down to a hanging position.

  o Switching your grip (front/back/side) will allow you to work on different muscle groups. For example, switching your grip to where your palms are facing in will focus on your biceps. This grip changes  the exercise name from a "pull up" to a "chin up." While hanging, try raising your knees up to your chest. This is an exercise that will work on your abdominal muscles. Your abs will also be working during a regular pull up to help stabilize your body.

  o There have even become popular workout routines that focus on using only pull up bars. It is a tremendous full-body exercise that you can tailor to meet your specific needs. Can't do a pull up? Once again don't worry! There are plenty of ways to build up to it and still work those muscles!

- o Need help? Try placing a chair beneath the bar and stand on it. Use the chair to help boost yourself over the bar with a jump. Once you're above the bar, slowly go down. Remember, when I was in high school, I could only do one pull up with a frontwards grip. Now I can do eighteen pull ups! I could only do thirty pushups in two minutes in high school. Now I can do over 100! If you work hard and stay consistent you will improve. To work on strengthening your muscles for pull ups, try having a spotter help you get over the bar.

- **Bicep Curls**: Hold the weight (whether free weight, machine, or homemade) with your arms extended and hanging at your side. There are multiple ways to perform bicep curls (each way slightly changes the area of the bicep worked). With your arms starting at your sides, curl your forearm towards your chest while twisting your wrist so your palm is facing your chest.

  - o Your bicep is the muscle on the top of your arm in-between your elbow and shoulder. Try to focus the lift solely on the bicep as you raise the weight to your chest and then lower back down to the starting position.
  - o Instead of twisting the weight, you can start with your palms facing out and the weight held in front of you.

Once again, curl your arm into your chest and then extend back down to the starting position. Make sure you go through the full range of motion!

- **Triceps extension**: You can perform this exercise lying down on a bench or in a standing position. Hold the weight behind your head with your arms bent. Start out with a low weight until you get the hang of this exercise to prevent injury.

  ○ Begin the exercise with your arms bent down low with your elbows in and then extend your arms upward until they are straight. Make sure you don't move the rest of your body to lift the weight. You should feel the burn in your triceps (the bottom muscle in your arm below the biceps).

- **Front raises**: Hold the weight with your arms in front of you and your knuckles facing outward. Raise the weight up to right below your chin and then lower back down to the starting position (your elbows will bend out as you raise the weight upward).

- **Lateral raise**: Stand holding a weight at either side (start with very light weight!). Raise your arms up laterally until they are parallel to your shoulders (almost like jumping jacks but don't go as high up). This exercise will work your latissimus dorsi muscle.

- **Shoulder press**: Sit down with your back against a chair/bench. If necessary, you may do this exercise from a standing position, but you must be careful to keep your back straight. Start by holding the weight right above your shoulders. Extend your arms straight upward and raise the weight until your arms are extended before lowering the weight back down. This exercise will help build up your deltoid muscles.

- **Shrugs**: Hold a weight in each hand with your arms extended at your sides. While keeping your arms straight, roll your shoulders either forward or to the rear. This is another great shoulder exercise!

- **Flys**: Lie down flat on a bench. Start by holding a weight in each hand with your arms up towards the ceiling in an extended position. Bring the weights close together so that they are touching (turn your wrists if using free weights so that they can come closer together). The motion for this exercise is similar to giving someone a big hug.
    - o Slowly lower the weights out towards your sides until they are parallel with your body or a little below. Once the weights reach this point, explode in an inward and upward motion to bring the weights back together. This exercise will squeeze your pec muscles to bring the weights inward.

LEG EXERCISES

- **Squats**: One of the most effective leg exercises. Start in a standing position with your legs shoulder width apart. Slowly bend your legs until you are near a 90 degree angle (don't go to 90 degrees unless you are experienced) between your upper torso and upper leg. It is IMPERATIVE that you keep your back straight during this exercise!
    - o Don't lean forward since this will put unnecessary stress on your back. To accomplish this, try holding your arms out in front of you to help you balance. If you're still having trouble, put your back against a wall or an exercise ball. This will force you to keep your back straight throughout the exercise.

- o Do squats hurt your knees? If this is the case, don't go down as far. Do a slight motion and keep your speed at a low intensity to prevent injury. Squats work on many major muscle groups, including your quadriceps, hamstrings, and glutes. They are one of the most complete leg exercises.

- o There are many variations to this exercise. Try turning your feet outwards at a 45 degree angle like a duck (legs are still shoulder width apart.) Another challenge is to stay on your toes the whole time as you perform the movement. Try getting into a squat position, holding for 10 seconds, and then coming back up. Or try twisting in the squat position (like a skier) or pulsing (short up and down movements near 90 degrees before fully returning to the starting position).

- **Lunges**: Lunges are a personal favorite for working the lower body. Similar to the squat in effectiveness, this exercise works on many different muscle groups in your lower body (hamstrings, quadriceps, and glutes).

  - o Start in a standing position. Take a step out with either foot and slowly lower yourself to the ground until your knee is almost touching the ground. If you feel tension on the joints instead of the muscle, then don't go down as far. You also might be stepping out too far or too short, so experiment with a comfortable and natural step forward.

  - o Once your knee is near the ground, shift your weight to your front foot and step out with the other foot. Repeat the process and lower your body with the opposite foot forward. Find an area where you can walk/lunge for at least a few steps before having to turn around.

○ If you don't have space to walk, you can come back to a standing position in-between and remain in place. However, many people find that this technique puts more stress on their joints and there is a break in the muscle tension.

○ Are lunges too easy for you? The military introduced me to a fantastic alternative to this exercise. Perform a regular lunge, but once your knee is near the ground, explosively jump upward! While you're in the air, switch which leg is facing forward. As you land, immediately go into the lunge with the opposite leg and then explode back into a jump once your knee is near the ground.

○ Continue to alternate feet as you perform jumping lunges. This is a fantastic exercise to build power, speed, and explosion. It will also fatigue you a lot faster than regular lunges and can be used as a high intensity exercise.

- **Side raises**: Lie on your side with one of your hands holding your head up. While keeping the rest of your body motionless and in a straight line, raise your leg up sideways into the air as far as you can. Slowly lower your leg back down and repeat. You might not feel this exercise right away but it will burn after a minute! Once you have reached muscular failure, switch sides and do the opposite leg.

- **Mountain climbers**: This is a spectacular leg, core, and cardio exercise. Start out with both knees on the ground and your hands on the ground in front of you (underneath your shoulders). Use your hands to hold the weight of your body and curl one of your legs forward while straightening out the other leg behind you. Balance yourself on the toes of your feet.

o Now that you're in the starting position, begin to alternate the positions of your legs. As you bring one leg to your chest, you should be straightening out the other leg behind you. This is a great full body exercise and another favorite of the military.

- **High knee jumps**: Jump up and down as high as you can while bringing your knees up to your chest each time. Wait...that's it? Yep. That's all there is to this exercise and yet it's extremely effective. This is a great exercise to increase your leg explosion along with your maximum jump height. High knee jumps are also a great cardio exercise and you will feel your heart rate increase rapidly.

- **Dot drill**: Dot drill is one of my favorite agility exercises. Not only are you building agility and quick feet, but you are strengthening your legs at the same time. Place tape, dots, cardboard, or any flat object on the ground in the pattern of what the number five looks like on a dice. Two dots in the front, two in the back, and one in the middle.

  o Create patterns where you hop from dot to dot with two feet, one foot, or with different feet at each dot. The one-legged hops are awesome for building power in your legs and maximizing your ability to change direction quickly. Try timing yourself in a routine you design so you can measure your improvement.

o   If you are overweight, I would avoid this exercise since it puts too much weight on one foot and could be dangerous. Focus on exercises that do not have as much jumping.

ABDOMINAL CORE EXERCISES

- **Flutter kicks and Leg lifts**: Lie flat on your back with your legs straight out in front of you. Slide both your hands underneath your waist and under your butt. Putting your arms in this position will help you not injure your back and give added support. If you want a challenge and have strong abdominal muscles, try this exercise without the support of your arms underneath you.

    o   Sit up slightly and you're ready to begin the exercise! You should be looking at your toes, not the ceiling. Raise your legs 6 inches off the ground. During this exercise, never let your legs touch the ground but return them to 6 inches each time, alternately kicking your legs into the air like you were swimming or walking with them.

    o   For a variation of this exercise, keep both legs together and raise them up to a 90 degree angle before returning them to 6 inches. You will feel your abdominal muscles stretch and burn along with some of your leg muscles. Another variation is to spread your legs outwards to the side instead of raising them up or to perform a scissor kick with them.

    o   For more of a challenge, pretend your toes are the tip of a pencil and try writing your name in big letters. This will work both your obliques and your rectus abdominis muscle.

- **V sit-ups**: V sit-ups are an advanced abdominal exercise. Lie flat on your back and extend your arms out behind your head. In one fluid motion, bring your lower body and upper body together and touch your hands to your toes. Your body should make a "V" shape as you bring the two halves of your body together.

- **Sit-ups**: Sit-ups are a foundation of any abdominal program and are part of the Army Physical Fitness Test. Try performing this exercise without having anyone hold your feet. This will target the exercise more onto your abdominal muscles. If a spotter holds your feet, you will be able to use your hips and legs to help.

  o Start by lying flat on the ground with your legs curled in towards your chest. Keep your feet on the ground and have a spotter hold them if you can't perform the exercise on your own, or you want to work on your hips and legs as well. If you don't have anyone to spot you, try putting your feet underneath a couch or another heavy object you can safely squeeze them under.

  o Put your hands behind your head or across your chest. Raise your torso up until your arms touch your legs or until you are "sitting up." Lower back down until your shoulder blades touch the ground and then repeat.

- **Rock climbers**: This is an exercise that I made up on my own. It probably has an actual name but I like to call them "rock climbers" because that's what I pretend to do when I perform them. Start in a raised sit up position. Slowly let your torso lower to the ground until your shoulder blades are almost touching. Remain in this position and use your abs to hold yourself there while you begin to pretend to rock climb.

o Extend your arms in an alternating fashion behind your head. Every now and then, raise a leg to your chest, or pretend to reach out for a handhold to the side. Whatever you do, continue to utilize your abdominal muscles to hold yourself off the ground.

High Intensity Weight Loss at Home

Remember that one of the biggest keys to losing weight is to perform high intensity workouts that involve strength training. These workouts keep your heart rate up, involve strength training, push you to your limit, and maximize the afterburn effect. Many of the above exercises are perfect to include in these workouts since they work on your strength. However, not all of these exercises keep your heart rate at a super high level.

To achieve a high heart rate throughout your workout, you want to include exercises that are tailored for this. Once your heart rate is up, go back to a strength exercise. Even though you are still exercising, your heart rate will decrease since strength exercise is not as fast-paced.

After one or two strength exercises, return immediately to an exercise that elevates your heart rate. Repeat this pattern and you have a high-intensity workout that is optimal for weight loss! Below are some exercises that are great for increasing your heart rate in a short amount of time.

- **Jumping Jacks**: Jumping jacks are a great warm-up exercise and a great way to elevate your heart rate. Start in a standing position with your arms at your side. At the same time, jump into the air and spread your feet and arms out. Bring your arms all the way above your head to where you could clap your hand together if you wanted to. Return to the starting position and repeat immediately. Perform these at a fast pace and your heart will race.

- **Sprints**: Sprinting in between sets of strength exercises is a fantastic way to keep the workout intense. If you have a nearby hill, use that to increase the difficulty even further. To change it up, try variations such as backpedaling, shuffling, or jumping.
    - o Do all of these exercises as fast as you can. If you are at home, sprint in place and bring your knees up to your chest (high knees). Run in place rapidly and you will be surprised at how much your heart rate increases. The key is pushing yourself as hard as you can.
- **Burpees**: Burpees are one of the best full body exercises that you can perform at home without any equipment. Start in the standing position. Your first step is to squat down and place your hands on the ground like you were a frog (feet on the ground, legs bent, and hands on the ground). Your next step is to place your weight on your hands as you jump your legs out behind you into a pushup position.
    - o Perform one pushup, and then spring your legs back into the frog position. Stand back up and jump high into the air with your arms above your head. Once you land, repeat the exercise. This high-intensity exercise works many different muscle groups and will burn you after only a few repetitions!

You have now learned multiple exercises that you can perform right in your own home! There is no excuse for not taking care of the body that God gave you. Even if you are only able to work out for twenty minutes a day, stay consistent and you will begin to see a difference. These home workouts will help you have a strong healthy body that is ready to excel in all that God has called you to do!

Chapter 11

CARDIO WORKOUTS

Building Cardiovascular/Cardiorespiratory Endurance

E ver wished that you could run 2 miles, 5 miles, or 20 miles? Completing an endurance event like this is a measure of your cardiovascular and cardiorespiratory endurance. One of the mighty men of David certainly possessed this physical trait. 2 Samuel

2:18 tells us that "Asahel was as swift footed as one of the gazelles which is in the field." His endurance likely aided him in many of the battles that he fought with King David.

Your aerobic capacity is determined by your cardiovascular/ cardiorespiratory endurance. These terms are often used interchangeably even though they are slightly different. The term "cardiovascular" refers more to your heart, while the term "cardiorespiratory" refers more to your lungs. Both of these terms are describing the ability of your body to provide and absorb oxygenated blood. The heart, lungs, veins, and arteries must all work together to make this phenomenon possible.

Your heart contains cardiac muscle that can become stronger through physical activity. Just like your skeletal muscles, your heart will adjust to the demand you are placing upon it. The more you exercise, the better your heart becomes at pumping out blood to the rest of the body. This is seen by an increase in "stroke volume" (the amount of blood pumped out by each beat of the heart.)

If your heart is more efficient at pumping out blood, it doesn't have to beat as fast to provide oxygenated blood to your muscles. This means that through training, your heart won't beat as fast to exercise at the same intensity. Due to this factor, you can exercise at higher intensities and you don't fatigue as quickly. Workouts that are long in duration (and keep the heart at an elevated heart rate) are especially effective at increasing your stroke volume.

Not only will physical exercise be easier, but this is a benefit to your body at rest, too! Your body will be more efficient at providing needed nutrients and oxygen to your body throughout your day! This can lead to increased energy, improved mood, and improved mental capacity.

Cardio workouts will also raise your body's ability to utilize the oxygenated blood that the heart is supplying. Oxygen is vital in helping the body create ATP (adenosine triphosphate) or energy to maintain prolonged physical activity. This process is measured through your V02 max (the maximal volume of oxygen that your body can utilize).

Research has shown that physical training can increase a person's VO2 max. Through training, you are now pumping out more blood per heartbeat and you have increased your body's ability to utilize the oxygen in that blood!

Preventing Injury

Before you sprint away from this book to go get a cardio workout in, you should know some basics to prevent injury. First of all, make sure you have the right equipment. For example, if you're a runner, make sure you buy some good running shoes. Having improper footwear can quickly lead to an impact injury such as "shin splints." While footwear helps, prayer is your best weapon to prevent injury or to heal it.

During my senior year of football, I got terrible shin splints during the first two weeks of practice. I was in shape, but my legs were not used to the constant pounding of slamming my feet to the ground as I ran pass routes. The force generated from rapidly changing direction and making quick cuts began to take a toll on my shins.

It wasn't long before I had sharp pain shooting up my shins every time I increased my pace from walking. Missing practice was NOT an option to me. I was determined to play my senior year and not fall behind. Most people would tell you that continuing to train with shin splints would only make them worse. However, instead of resting, I just prayed for my shin splints to go away.

We had a scrimmage at the end of the week. I went from having sharp, dramatic pain in my shins to the pain being completely gone when scrimmage day came. The pain never returned. It wasn't a gradual lessening of the pain, but rather a miracle from God where the pain completely vanished.

Now that I've learned about praying in faith, I cover myself in prayer. If I feel the slightest pain in my legs, I declare that it has to go in Jesus' name! While you have the power through faith in Jesus' name to heal, you should still use wisdom and get some good running shoes. Who you are in Christ doesn't mean that you "test God" and neglect wisdom.

If you are continuing to experience pain from running, try mixing up your workouts with swimming or elliptical machines. Both of these cardio workouts are "low impact" and won't put the same type of force/stress on your joints.

Find safe routes to run on. People have died from running on dangerous roads where a car crested a hill too fast or didn't have time to react. You should wear bright colors, find a running buddy, warm up, and hydrate properly.

Types and Frequency of Cardio Workouts

Most cardio workouts are moderate in intensity and won't break down your muscles as much as a high intensity workout (such as strength training). Due to this, you can perform cardio workouts frequently without having to worry about overtraining your muscles. Instead of muscles not recovering, the threat of overtraining with cardio is too much impact/stress on joints, tendons, or ligaments.

While most cardio workouts are at a low intensity, it is still possible to rev up this intensity through maximal effort. When cardio is performed at a high intensity, it begins to become more of an anaerobic activity. This technique is often used by athletes seeking top performance in a given sport.

Even distance athletes will often include high intensity training sessions into their workout regimen to gain the edge when they need it, allowing them to exert maximal energy to run away from the pack on a bike race, gain the lead in a swimming event, or finish strong in the last lap of a long race. These intense bursts of energy will often leave your muscles exhausted. You will likely find that your body responds better from having a lighter day of training or a rest day after pushing yourself to your max.

Remember the principles of fitness from earlier in this book as they apply to cardio workouts as well. The more you perform cardio workouts, the stronger your cardiovascular and cardiorespiratory system become. It's the law of sowing and reaping. When you begin to plateau, increase your speed or the duration of the workout (principle of overload). If you stay consistent, you will progress and get better. Everyone's body is different, so find the frequency and length of workout that fits your body type and lifestyle.

There are many different types of cardio workouts! Running, swimming, and biking are perhaps the most popular, but there are many others. Certain types of sports, hiking, video workouts, and games can be cardio workouts, too. Find activities that you enjoy. Running for two hours a day isn't for everyone.

I would much rather get a cardio benefit from playing a sport and having fun. Or, if I have to work out by myself, I prefer an intense sprinting session that only takes me a half hour and is tailored more to build power and speed. But that's just me. You don't have to be someone else. You just have to be the best "you" that you can be.

Speed Workouts

Want to build speed? Countless activities rely on this skill component. Speed is a product of power. The formula for power is force x acceleration. To gain speed, you should perform exercises that are fast, short in duration, explosive, intense, and have some form of resistance. This type of training will also build Type II muscle fibers (fast twitch). Remember that these fibers respond quicker and produce more power.

Sprints, weight training, running up stadium steps or a hill, and box jumps are examples of physical activities that help build speed. To build speed, you train with speed. Once you are warmed up, focus on fast repetitions with moderate resistance. For example, try an all-out sprint with a parachute dragging behind you. Or, try pushing a sled for 10 yards, relaxing for 15 seconds, and then pushing it again another 10 yards (repeat).

If you need some other type of resistance, try wearing a weighted vest, or having a friend hold your waist and pull back while you run forward. If you're by yourself, just find a steep hill. The added incline will strain your muscles as you run up backwards, sideways, regular, and even on all fours.

Agility and quick feet drills are another fantastic way to build speed. These drills focus on short bursts of speed in multiple directions. Cone drills (running or performing a type of movement between cones) dot drills (hopping/jumping from one spot to another repeatedly or in patterns), and plyometrics are all examples of this.

Plyometrics incorporate many different agility drills that aid in developing proper running form. They are very popular in dynamic warm up routines and help the muscles transition quickly between concentric and eccentric movements. Examples of plyometrics include power skips, karaoke, lunges, backpedalling, sprints, shuffling, and high knees.

WORKOUT CHARTS

If you're at this point in the book, then you have read a lot about physical fitness! How do you apply all of that information? While I encourage you to reread sections that apply specifically to you, I also thought I would give you some basic workout charts depending on your fitness goal. Feel free to adjust them to meet your individual needs and body type.

If the load is too heavy, or you are just starting out, add a day of rest in-between each workout day. You can also reduce the frequency to only "once per day." If the load is too light and you are not seeing results, add a longer duration to each workout or increase your intensity.

If you are building you own chart, try the formula FITT (Frequency, Intensity, Time, Type). In other words, figure out "how often," "how hard," "how long," and "what type" each workout will be. For tips and procedures to complete the workouts, refer to the previous sections.

Strength Workout Example

Day	Muscle Group	Time/ Frequency	Type/Intensity
Monday	Chest/ Shoulders/Back	70 minutes x1	Heavy weight 80 to 90 percent max
Tuesday	Legs and Abs plus speed workout	90 minutes x 1	Power training for speed, core workouts, then 80 to 90 percent max on legs
Wednesday	Biceps/Triceps	70 minutes x 1	Heavy weight 80 to 90 percent max
Thursday	Legs and Abs plus speed workout	90 minutes x 1	High intensity/ 70–80 percent max, Sets to failure
Friday	Chest/ Shoulders/Back	70 minutes x 1	70–80 percent max
Saturday	Biceps/Triceps	60 minutes x 1	70 to 80 percent max
Sunday	OFF	OFF	OFF

Weight Loss Example Workout

*There are two workouts for most days (cardio plus high intensity).
Complete one in the morning and one in the evening
(work up to this, start out with fewer days)

Day	Muscle Group	Time/ Frequency	Type/Intensity
Monday	All muscle groups plus cardio	-50 minutes all muscle groups x 1 -45 minutes cardio x 1	High intensity, low weight, high reps, keep heart rate up, include strength training in-between exercises to boost heart rate
Tuesday	Upper Split (Arms) plus cardio	-50 minutes Upper Split x 1 -45 minutes cardio x 1	High intensity, low weight, high reps, keep heart rate up, include strength training in-between exercises to boost heart rate
Wednesday	Lower Split (Legs and Abs) plus cardio	-50 minutes Lower Split x 1 -45 minutes cardio x 1	High intensity, low weight, high reps, keep heart rate up, include strength training in-between exercises to boost heart rate
Thursday	Upper split (Arms) plus cardio	-50 minutes Upper Split x 1 -45 minutes cardio x 1	High intensity, low weight, high reps, keep heart rate up, include strength training in-between exercises to boost heart rate

Friday	Lower Split (Legs and Abs) plus cardio	-50 minutes Lower Split x 1 -45 minutes cardio x 1	High intensity, low weight, high reps, keep heart rate up, include strength training in-between exercises to boost heart rate
Saturday	Fun Sports Day	80 minutes x 1	Do a physical activity or sport of your choice
Sunday	OFF	OFF	OFF

Example Cardiovascular Workout

Day	Activity	Time/ Frequency	Type/Intensity
Monday	Running	90 minutes x 1	Cardio (low to moderate)
Tuesday	Swimming	60 minutes x 1	Cardio (low to moderate)
Wednesday	Biking	90 minutes x 1	Cardio (low to moderate)
Thursday	Running	45 minutes x 2	Cardio (high intensity)
Friday	Sports	90 minutes x 1	Cardio sport of your choice
Saturday	Elliptical	45 minutes x 2	Cardio (low to moderate)
Sunday	OFF	OFF	OFF
Monday	Biking	45 minutes x 2	Cardio (high intensity)
Tuesday	Swimming	90 minutes x 1	Cardio (low to moderate)
Wednesday	Running	60 minutes x 2	Cardio (low to moderate)
Thursday	Biking	120 minutes	Cardio (low to moderate)
Friday	Sports	90 minutes x 1	Cardio
Saturday	Elliptical	60 minutes x 2	Cardio
Sunday	OFF	OFF	OFF

Example Cross Training Workout

Day	Muscle Group	Time/ Frequency	Type
Monday	All muscle groups	70 minutes x1	Circuit/Lift to failure (70 to 80 percent max)
Tuesday	Upper Split (Arms)	45 minutes x 2	Lift to failure/High reps (60 percent max)
Wednesday	Lower Split (Legs)	45 minutes x 2	Drop sets/Lift to failure/(60 percent max)
Thursday	Abs/Legs	45 minutes x 1	Abs plus sprint/speed workout
Friday	All/Sports	60 minutes x 1	Sports
Saturday	Running/ cardio	120 minutes x 1	Cardio/low intensity
Sunday	OFF	OFF	OFF
Monday	Chest/ Shoulders	40 minutes x 1	Heavy weight (80–90 percent max)
Tuesday	Biceps/ Triceps	40 minutes x 1	Heavy weight (80–90 percent max)
Wednesday	Legs/Abs	40 minutes x 2	Heavy weight (80–90 percent max)
Thursday	Swimming/ cardio	60 minutes x 1	Cardio/moderate intensity
Friday	Speed workout	45 minutes x 2	Sprints/Stairs/ Plyometrics
Saturday	All muscle groups	80 minutes x 1	High intensity circuit (70 percent max)
Sunday	OFF	OFF	OFF

Workout Music

Do you need some extra motivation during your workout? Many people enjoy working out to music. The beat or lyrics of a song can inspire you to drive past the pain and push harder than you thought you could.

However, it's very important to listen to the RIGHT kind of music. I don't care how good of a beat a song has... if the song has bad lyrics, don't listen to it. If the song is written by an artist who lives an immoral lifestyle, don't listen to it. If the song curses, tears down, or says negative things, DON'T LISTEN TO IT!

Music has a big influence on how you think. Your thinking will then have an impact on how you actually act. Proverbs 23:7 says, "For as he thinks within himself, so he is." If you listen to negative lyrics, you will begin to think and act according to what you hear.

What kind of words are you hearing? Would you rather sow life or death into your mind? "Faith comes by hearing, and hearing by the word of Christ."—Romans 10:17. Instead of listening to junk, listen to songs that line up with the Word of God and build your faith!

I have found that I'm most motivated by Christian music. This is because my true fulfillment is found in Christ. Christian music motivates me to work hard for God instead of for myself. I'm taking care of the temple He gave me and the platform by which I preach His gospel. My love for Him shifts me into a whole new level of motivation and drive. Every repetition has meaning. Christian music can help me step into His presence while working out. If I don't have music, then I declare His Word in-between sets.

Wait a minute.... Is there Christian music that is actually good? Christian music has exploded and is better now than it ever has been. Not just good lyrics, but good beats as well! I believe this is part of the outpouring of God's Spirit that He is doing in these last days.

Haven't heard good Christian music before? Don't give up. Search the style of music you like and you will be surprised at the variety of Christian artists that have taken the stage. There are plenty of good beats with lyrics that are speaking life.

Here's a list of my personal favorite top 15 workout albums! Included are the album, the artist, and the type of style (at least how the style sounds to me). Try some of these albums out or search for your own.

My Favorite "Top 15" Albums for Working Out

1. **We are Young and Free** (Hillsong Young and Free) (Pop/Praise)
2. **Royal Flush** (Flame) Rap
3. **This is Not a Test** (Toby Mac) (Pop)
4. **Capitol Kings** (Capitol Kings) (Rock/Techno/Pop)
5. **Time Stands Still** (Family Force 5) (Rock)
6. **Rehab** (Lecrae) (Rap)
7. **Restart** (Newsboys) (Rock)
8. **6th Day** (Flame) (Rap)
9. **Awakening Live from Chicago** (Jesus Culture) (Praise and Worship)
10. **Born Again** (Newsboys) Rock
11. **Gold** (Britt Nicole) Pop
12. **Ready to Fly** (Jamie Grace) (Pop)
13. **Awake** (Skillet) Hard Rock
14. **Chronicles of an X-Hustler** (Thi'sl) (Rap)
15. **Life** (Beckah Shae) (Pop)
16. **Horseshoes and Handgrenades** (Disciple) (Hard Rock)

You are set and ready to start working out! You understand why it's important as a Christian to workout, how to win the battle inside your mind, how to use your faith, how to apply fitness and spiritual principles, and how to conduct the actual workouts! Congratulations!

However, there is a final key we must address for you to have success in your training. That key...is nutrition. Skipping this key will shortchange your workouts and hinder any progress. Applying this key will accelerate you to whichever fitness goal you are trying to achieve.

Chapter 12

Keys to Nutrition

N
utrition goes hand in hand with physical activity in taking care of the body that God gave you. Your intense workout can be negated in minutes by eating unhealthily. Whether you are trying to maximize performance, increase the

health-related components of physical fitness, lose weight, or feel energized, you need to eat properly!

God-made food vs. man-made food

When I'm training clients, the people who achieve fitness goals are the ones whos are eating healthy along with our workouts. They have incorporated the most essential key to proper nutrition: eating food the way God made it.

Much of the food you find in the grocery store today has been altered by man with extra chemicals, preservatives, and genetic modifications. This process has removed much of the nutritional value from the food and replaced it with junk that acts as poison to your body.

This poison can turn off your body's fat burning switch. It can also make you lose energy, make you feel dependent upon the poison itself, and can lead to numerous short-term and long-term health-related problems.

Remember the law of sowing and reaping? If you sow destruction into your body, then your body is going to reap destruction. If you sow healthy foods into your body, then your body is going to reap life.

The closer a food is to its natural state, the healthier that food is going to actually be for your body. When God made the plants and animals, "He saw it was good." The nutrients from these plants and animals are good for your body and designed to be digested and processed. Your body easily filters out the nutrients it needs and gets rid of the waste.

But throw in some added chemicals and preservatives, and now your body doesn't know how to break the food down. This leads your body to store much of this food as fat. Not to mention the harmful chemicals that are now in your bloodstream, the excessive amount of fat or sugar you digested from the food, and the increased insulin level you are developing from removing the sugar.

On top of all the negative side effects of man-altered food, you only receive minimal actual nutrition from these foods. This can quickly lead to overeating in an attempt to satisfy the lack of nutrients that your body is suffering from.

Does this mean that you can never eat a food that has chemicals added to it? Not at all! It would be very hard to accomplish this in a world where the majority of our food is modified. But you should make a real effort to eat as natural as possible. You don't need chemicals to enjoy fruits, vegetables, meats, dairy, and grains. You can enjoy all of these food groups in their created state and get the maximal nutritional boost that God designed. Changing your diet to REAL food can make an immediate impact on your health, body composition, and life.

Preparation Ensures Participation

My pastor often says that "preparation ensures participation." He is referring to being clothed in readiness so that you can always step into what God has for you. It's not time to get ready, it's time to be ready. It's hard to step out in faith if you have never taken the time to develop it. This same principle is true for your participation in healthy eating.

If you're going to participate in healthy eating, you need to prepare for it. If you walk into your kitchen and all you see is snacks, then there is a problem. You have created an unhealthy environment where temptation is lurking at every corner. Instead, your kitchen should be filled with healthy, nutrient-rich food. This will greatly increase the chance of you actually eating or making a healthy meal.

Unhealthy food is quick and easy to make. Not buying it in the first place is your best defense against eating too much of it. When you go to the grocery store, try to stay out of the middle aisles and patrol the perimeter. The perimeter is often where all of the natural foods are.

Plan out what you will eat each week. You are less likely to buy junk if your mind is already made up on the healthy foods you are planning to buy. The military taught me that "failing to plan is planning to fail." If you're trying to save money, check out buying healthy food in bulk at stores like Costco. Or look for the sales.

I often look for sales on chicken. A different cut or type is usually on sale if you buy in bulk (sometimes at 59 cents a pound!) Cook up as much of the chicken as you can when you get home and eat it throughout the week as a healthy snack. If you bought too much, then store the additional uncooked chicken in the freezer.

FOOD AS A BLESSING, NOT AN IDOL

Food is a wonderful blessing from God. It nourishes our bodies, gives us joy as we taste it, and provides us opportunity to share and partake in fellowship as we eat. However, you can't be filled up on just food. Deut. 8:3 says, "Man does not live by bread alone, but man lives by everything that proceeds out of the mouth of the Lord."

Food may gratify your hunger, but God is the only One who can truly fill you up. Worldly things only gratify; God satisfies. God is the True Bread, the Living Water, the One who gives you life and life abundantly! You need to be filled up with His Word and not just food. That's what will truly strengthen and empower you.

Food must never be put above God. An idol is anything that is put up in the place of God. Just because you don't have a statue in your house that you bow down to doesn't mean that you don't have idols in your life. People worship singers, actors, food, sports, themselves, and many other things. It's okay to like and enjoy things, but you can't ever put them above your walk with God.

God wants to be first in EVERY area of your life. You are to have "no other gods before Me."—Deut. 5:7. Don't let food become something that you worship. Don't let it become a stumbling block that you constantly give into. If food has become master over you, then it has turned into an idol. This downward path can quickly lead a person into gluttony or eating disorders. Paul tells us in Romans 6 to not let sin be a master over us. He later tells the church at Corinth to not be mastered by anything (1 Corinthians 6:12).

You have the ability to control your mind, will, and emotions. You don't have to compromise with overeating or unhealthy food. You don't have to settle for food being in control of you instead of the other way around. God has given you victory in Christ! Be led by your Spirit and not by your flesh. Speak His Word, declare it when you feel like eating unhealthily, and watch how your mind is renewed and every thought is brought captive to Christ.

Proportion Size

Overeating is one of the biggest culprits in obesity and weight gain. Most people understand that eating too much over the period of a day will cause you to gain weight. If you take in more calories in a day than you expend, you will store the extra amount. What some people don't understand is that overeating during ONE meal can cause you to gain weight. It's important to eat in the proper proportions!

Your body can only utilize so much energy at one time. Overeating during one meal will cause your body to store the extra amount. It would be healthier to eat a total of 3,000 calories in several meals throughout a day than to eat 2,500 calories in one meal and then starve yourself the rest of the day. Your body will store the extra amount from the meal in which you overate and won't burn any of it the rest of the day since you're starving yourself. Starving and going on yo-yo diets will only cause your body to store what it has due to its survival instinct. On the other hand, eating every few hours will help to rev up your metabolism.

Think you're losing weight by skipping breakfast? Totally wrong! Breakfast is actually the meal in which you should be eating the most. It will give you the energy to make it through the day and you will have burned most of it off by the night. Rather than having giant-proportion size meals, try having smaller meals six times a day. Or have three main meals with a snack in-between each meal.

Mastering Your Mind and Appetite

There is a big difference between hunger and appetite. Hunger is a natural feeling associated with the need for food. Appetite, on the other hand, is a want or desire for food. Sometimes we don't really need food, but our lustful desire for it drives us to continue to eat anyway. Instead of stopping with the normal proportion, your appetite tells you, "Keep going!" It's important to learn to control your appetite along with the mindset that goes with it. You can't let your appetite turn into lustful greed.

Not mastering your appetite and letting your lustful desire drive you can get you into trouble real quick. We find an example of this when Israel was in the wilderness. After being delivered from slavery in Egypt, by many signs and wonders the people of Israel continued to doubt and test God. Their lustful desire and greed led them to grumble and complain about food and water rather than trusting in God for provision.

God told the people that He would "rain bread from heaven for you, and the people shall go out and gather a day's portion every day," —Exodus 16:4. This bread was called "manna," which is the Hebrew term for "what is it?" The people had never encountered this bread from heaven before. This supernatural provision continued all the years that Israel was in the wilderness until the day that Joshua led them into the Promised Land.

What an amazing miracle from God! Imagine having your food fall from heaven every day for you! And yet Israel's lack of faith and lustful desire drove them to continue to test God. They complained about the manna and said that "our appetite is gone. There is nothing at all to look at except this manna."—Numbers 11:6. They grumbled that they had better food in Egypt and questioned and doubted God.

Nothing is too hard for God, and he sent a wind that "brought quail from the sea, and let them fall beside the camp, about a day's journey on this side and a day's journey on the other side, all around the camp and about two cubits deep on the surface of the ground." Can you picture how much quail this is?! A cubit is about a foot and a half in today's measurements. We are talking about quail piled up three feet high for miles around! God had just demonstrated again that He provides for His people and that nothing is impossible for Him.

But instead of learning their lesson, the people of Israel gather the quail like they will never see it again. In a greedy manner, they spend all day, all night, and all day the next day gathering! He who gathers the least gathered ten homers (which is ten piles!). Why the greedy and lustful rush? If God provided this time, don't you know that He will provide again?

"While the meat was still between their teeth, before it was chewed, the anger of the Lord was kindled against the people, and the Lord struck the people with a severe plague. So the name of that place was called Kibroth-hattaavah (the graves of greediness) because there they buried the people who had been greedy."— Numbers 11:33–34. The book of Psalms gives us more insight on the event and states that the people "**craved intensely** in the wilderness, and tempted God in the desert"—Psalm 106:14.

It's okay to enjoy the food God gave you. It is a blessing from Him and meant for enjoyment. But don't be like Israel was in the wilderness and let your appetite begin to master you. Don't let greed turn into an intense craving that you have no control of. You have the mind of Christ and you possess your mind, will, and emotions. You have the victory in Christ to control your proportions and food choices.

WHAT ABOUT
GLUTTONY IN THE BIBLE?

When most Americans think of the word "gluttony," they think it refers to someone who is obese or overweight. This is not necessarily the case. While obesity is often the result of gluttony, gluttony itself is the action of greedily taking in more than you need or squandering away what you have. It's a desire to want more and more.

The word translated as "glutton" in the Bible is the Hebrew word "zalal." *Zalal* means to be "worthless" or to "squander away." This is why the book of Proverbs tells us, "Do not be with heavy drinkers of wine, or with gluttonous eaters of meat; for the heavy drinker and the glutton will come to poverty, and drowsiness will clothe one with rage."—Proverbs 23:20–21.

Gluttony deals more with how you are eating your food instead of the state derived from it. Have you been a glutton in the past? Has it led to negative outcomes in your life? If so, don't worry! Remember, you aren't defined by your past, and God has an awesome plan for your life! You don't have to be enslaved by gluttony or another addiction.

Break whatever it is off you in Jesus' name! God has called you for greatness and it's time for you to step out into His calling for you. It's hard to step out when you're shackled and have anchors dragging behind you—which is why **today is your day** to cut those chains and anchors off.

Moderation and Substitution

"It is not good to eat much honey"—Proverbs 25:27. Notice how this statement from the book of Proverbs didn't say to not eat honey at all. It's okay to have an occasional treat and enjoy some of your favorite foods. The key is to eat these foods in moderation.

Paul tells the Corinthians, "All things are lawful for me, but not all things are profitable. All things are lawful for me, but I will not be mastered by anything."— 1 Corinthians 6:12. Just because you are allowed to eat something doesn't mean that it's profitable to eat it all the time. For example, my family knows that I absolutely love milkshakes! On top of that, I love any food that has chocolate in it. While it's okay to enjoy the occasional milkshake or sweet treat, I must eat these foods in moderation because they are unhealthy. Eating these foods regularly would cause me to quickly gain fat, lose energy, and begin to crave more unhealthy food.

Are there certain foods that you are having a hard time separating from? Either break the addiction with the Word or find a healthy substitute. A healthy substitute was the perfect solution to calm my craving for milkshakes. My love for milkshakes has turned into a love for protein shakes. Combine a little protein powder with some ice, real fruit, and some milk and you have a shake that is much healthier than its ice cream counterpart.

Chapter 13

NUTRIENTS

Nutrients are substances in food that your body utilizes to grow, maintain, repair, and operate your body. They are the nourishment necessary for your body to function. Making sure your food intake contains the proper nutrients will allow you to optimize your health, physical fitness, and calling.

If you want to build muscle, then you are going to make sure your body is full of the protein to do so. If you want to run an endurance event, then you have to make sure your glycogen stores are maxed out from eating carbohydrates before the event. If you want to perform at your best during your average workday, then you have to make sure you have the energy from nutrients to accomplish this. If you want to prevent illness and disease in the first place, then your body's defense system should be built up from antioxidants. Nutrients are essential and it's important to understand the different types and classes.

Carbohydrates

Carbohydrates are organic compounds that make up the starches and sugars found in food. They are comprised of carbon, oxygen, and hydrogen. Carbohydrates are the body's preferred source of energy. As soon as you eat carbohydrates, the body begins to convert them into a simple sugar called glucose. Glucose is then used by the body to supply immediate energy.

Any carbohydrates that aren't converted into glucose are converted by the body into glycogen and then stored. These storehouses are mainly found in the muscles and liver; they store the glycogen until the body needs it to convert back into glucose for energy.

Carbohydrates that are taken in beyond the body's ability to store them as glycogen are stored by the body as fat. Carbohydrates can be converted into energy much quicker than fat. Fat is made up of a very complex form of triglycerides and has to be broken down into free fatty acids first. Due to this, carbohydrates are often utilized first by the body during exercise. However, fats ultimately supply more energy (9 calories per gram compared to carbohydrates' 4 calories per gram).

There are two main types of carbohydrates: simple and complex. Simple carbohydrates are rapidly converted into glucose, whereas complex carbohydrates are broken down slowly. Complex carbohydrates are much healthier for you. They are found in bread, pasta, vegetables, and rice.

Simple carbohydrates are found in fruit juice, soda, candy bars, and sweets. They are called simple because they have a chemical structure composed of only one or two sugars. They are often full of refined sugar (manmade, instead of natural sugar found in fruit), artificial sweeteners, or hidden sugar under a sneaky name (such as maltodextrin). While these sugars can give you a quick energy boost, they will often lead to a crash later. Sugar can be very addictive, impair your immune system, and make you fat. Sugar can cause your body to become dependent on burning sugar, cause you to create excess insulin, and can even negate some of your muscle growth.

Complex carbohydrates don't throw your body into a spike since they break down at a slower and even rate. They supply your body with a constant source of energy and don't have the negative side effects associated with the simple carbohydrates. They are full of nutritional value and are the foundation of your daily intake.

There are strategies to cut carbs in an effort to burn fat. High protein, low carb, and low fat diets exist and have been successful for some people. However, if you are physically active, then you need these carbohydrates for energy. And if you're looking to build muscle, then you will need them alongside your intake of protein.

Protein

Proteins are the building blocks of muscle, body cells, and tissue. They are made up of long chains of amino acids. Your body can manufacture up to 11 out of the 20 amino acids in protein. You get the other 9 amino acids from foods that contain protein. These other 9 amino acids are known as "essential amino acids" since you can only get them from your food.

A food that contains all 9 of these amino acids is known as a "complete protein" source. Examples of complete protein sources are fish, chicken, milk, eggs, and cheese. Examples of incomplete proteins are grains, nuts, and beans. Does this 'mean that you shouldn't be eating incomplete protein sources? Not at all! You just want to make sure that your diet includes enough sources of protein that you are getting all of the essential amino acids.

Since protein is the building block of muscle, it's very important to get enough protein in your diet if you are trying to increase your strength. For most people, eating about 1 gram of protein per pound of body weight is a good estimate to gain muscle mass. You could go below this and still see results, but a gram a pound is probably more optimal. So if you weigh 150 pounds, then you should eat 150 grams of protein per day to increase muscle mass. Of course, there are variations depending upon your body type and gender, so find what works for you.

If you are an elite athlete, or really looking for muscular hypertrophy, then you may want to target 1.5 grams of protein per pound of body weight. Going much higher than this doesn't seem to have any additional muscular benefit. So if you weigh 150 pounds, and are in an INTENSE strength training regimen, then you should target 225 grams of protein per day. Whoa, that's an enormous amount of protein! How are you going to fit that much protein into your diet?

Well, you certainly won't be able to do so if you are wasting calories on junk food. When you eat unhealthily, not only are you probably gaining fat, but you are depriving your body of the nutrients (like protein) that it's craving. What benefit is there to a killer workout if you don't give your body what it needs to recover? To get this much protein in your diet, break it up in small meals or snacks throughout the day. Your body can only take so much protein in at once anyway; the rest is just waste.

So please don't take those protein shakes that contain 100 grams of protein! You are wasting most of that shake. Shoot for around 30 at a time and spread it out. That way, your body has a constant intake of protein and will be able to feed your muscles consistently.

Are you not accustomed to that much protein? Don't worry; remember that for most people who are trying to gain strength, the ratio is around a gram per pound. If you're a female, then it is likely lower than that. If you're only looking to lose weight, or your goal is more cardio/endurance-based, then you could go substantially lower than this. However, muscle is more metabolically active than regular tissue, so building a little muscle won't hurt you in your goal to lose weight. If you remember from earlier, high intensity strength training is one of the most effective weight loss strategies.

So what are some good sources of protein? I'm glad you asked! Fish, chicken, other meats, nuts, milk, yogurt, eggs, beans, and cheese can all be good sources of protein. Fish is one of the best and offers a whopping amount of protein for only a few calories. I like to buy tuna packets since they are an easy snack and take no preparation to enjoy.

Buying some whey protein powder and making shakes is a great after-workout snack. They can be extremely tasty or extremely awful. You just need the right brand and blend it with the right ingredients. Protein shakes can also be very beneficial in the morning (since they have a little sugar) to push the protein into your muscles after they have been depleted from sleeping for eight hours.

There are two times where it's actually beneficial to have sugar: right when you wake up, and immediately following a workout. In both cases, you are trying to speed the protein into your muscles. I'm not saying to have a candy bar for breakfast. The more natural the sugar, the better it is for you, and you only need a little sugar for this effect anyway, not forty grams like you will find in a candy bar.

Turkey burgers and edamame are two of my other favorites. A grilled turkey burger is full of 30 grams of protein and can taste amazing! Bags of edamame (soybeans) can be bought in bulk and they come in nice microwavable bags. Just pop it in the microwave for a minute or two, throw in some salt for taste, and enjoy! This tiny vegetable is packed with protein and is a great couch snack. Other vegetables like broccoli are good sources of protein as well.

Eggs are a quick way to get protein in your body. They don't take long to cook, or you can eat them faster by making hard boiled eggs in bulk. Then you can just peel and eat. If you want to add some more protein to your shake, then try liquid egg whites. You can buy these in bulk as well to save money.

Chicken is a staple of many diets. It is packed with protein and healthy nutrients. Remember to buy chicken on sale and in bulk like we discussed previously. If you want a sweeter source of protein, try Greek yogurt. It is much healthier than regular yogurt and often contains 16 grams of protein per small container.

Fat

Many people shudder at this word. But not all fat is bad. In fact, fat is necessary for many bodily functions. It's too much fat or unhealthy fats that have led to the obesity crisis in America. Fats actually provide double the energy per gram than either carbohydrates or proteins. However, they are very complex in nature and take the longest to break down.

Fat can aid in bodily growth, transportation of vitamins through the blood, and help to keep your skin healthy. However, fats are recommended to only comprise about 20 percent of your daily caloric intake. For many people, this number is around 50 to 60 percent!

Fast food restaurants provide burgers that can contain over 60 grams of fat in one burger! Combine this with some fatty fries and a sugar-filled soda and you have a recipe for disaster! And that's not all. Much of the fat in the burger and fries is trans fat. Trans fats are created when unsaturated fats are converted into saturated fats through a process called hydrogenation. This process has no nutritional value, alters the chemical structure of the fat to an unnatural state, increases LDL (bad type of cholesterol), and is banned in countries like Denmark, Australia, and Switzerland!

Restaurants and companies utilize trans fats since they boost the taste of the food and increase shelf life. Avoid trans fat and other preservatives. They are a killer to any diet and a main culprit in obesity. Monitor your overall fat intake and choose foods that are low in fat or contain healthy fat. Most natural foods meet this criterion (for example, fish, vegetables, fruit, and grains).

Vitamins and Minerals

Vitamins and minerals are both micronutrients that are imperative for many bodily processes. Vitamins are organic compounds, while minerals are inorganic. Getting the proper amount of these nutrients will greatly enhance your health and everyday living. They can help your body digest and absorb nutrients, form healthy bones, form healthy teeth, prevent illness, metabolize protein, prevent infection, and repair cellular damage.

There are many different vitamins and minerals. Each one has unique benefits and characteristics. So how do you make sure you are getting enough of them—especially if you don't' know what each vitamin or mineral specializes in? To make it simple, make sure you are eating enough fruits and vegetables. These two food groups are loaded with vitamins, minerals, and phytonutrients that are essential for your body.

Fruits and vegetables are often bright in color due to the properties of the phytonutrients inside of them. Not only will adding color to your meals make them look more appeasing, but you will be adding in essential nutrients in the process!

Water

The Bible often uses water to symbolize life. Jesus is the only One who gives us living water. Out of our innermost beings should flow rivers of that life giving water to others (see John 7:38). In the book of Revelation we see the "river of the water of life, clear as crystal, coming from the throne of God and of the Lamb"—Revelation 22:1.

It's very fitting for water to symbolize life since God made the body very dependent upon it. Your body is dead without water, and it is spiritually dead without God. Only Jesus can wash away your sins, make you righteous, and fill you up with His Spirit. Water is essential to every function and process of the body. If you aren't drinking enough water, you might still be surviving, but your body is operating on limited resources. It is not functioning to its full capacity.

The easiest way to check to see if you are drinking enough water is by the color of your urine. It should be close to clear in color and have a slight tint of yellow. If your urine is dark yellow, then you are dehydrated and not drinking enough water. By drinking ample amounts of water, you will have more energy, your body will operate better, and you may find yourself eating in better proportions.

Often our bodies aren't really hungry, they are just thirsty. Try replacing any soda you drink with a glass of water. One simple change in your diet—from unhealthy drinks like soda, to healthy drinks like water and milk—can be the first step to getting your body back into shape.

Chapter 14

A Chosen Generation:
What the Future Holds

I n the book of Acts, when the Holy Spirit fell on the day of Pentecost, Peter boldly preached the gospel. Full of wisdom and revelation from the Holy Spirit, Peter's sermon led to three thousand people being saved that day. The gospel rapidly began to be spread throughout the nations. Everywhere the apostles went, signs and wonders followed as God confirmed their message. They did not come in words only, but in power and demonstration of the Holy Spirit.

This movement still continues today! Not only does it continue, but we are part of an end-time generation that will see God pour out His Spirit like never before!

Jesus isn't coming back for a run-down, divided up, broken-down bride. He is coming back for a Church that has made herself ready; a Church moving in love, power, and demonstration. I don't know the day that Jesus is coming back, but I do know that it is soon! We are seeing the signs and birth pains telling us what season we are in.

Whether Jesus comes back in a few years or in a hundred years, know that you are in the last days. And know that God has plans for you to do awesome things for Him!

This isn't the time to be lulled to sleep by entertainment. This isn't the time to be one of the ten virgins who didn't have their lamps lit. Don't tolerate sin or conform to the world. While most of the world is growing in sin and immorality, there is a remnant that is learning how to walk with God and be led by His Spirit.

It's time to wake up, put on the armor of God, and live for Him. Only you can fulfill the calling that He has for you. You are unique. There is no one else quite like you. Regardless of your vocation, God has called you to influence the people around you. Don't feel inadequate. God is the One who will strengthen you and be with you. He will redeem all of your gifts and talents and bring them out to His glory like never before!

Remember, you are called as an ambassador of Christ. To love, heal, deliver, set free, and preach to the nations. You don't have to wait for God to call you — He already has!

It's time to work out to reach out! Taking care of your body will allow you to maximize the calling and mission that God has for you. Take care of your temple and allow your body to glorify the Lord in all that you do. Offer it up to Him as a living sacrifice. Be filled with energy, joy, and good health. Your body is the vessel by which you will preach the gospel!

This book has shown you not only why you have to be physically fit, but how to get physically fit. My prayer is that this book helps you in your walk with God. That it breaks off any chains that were holding you back. That it helps you to know who you truly are in Christ. That it helps you take care of your body. That it helps you live by faith. That you, being full of energy, healthy and free of sickness, move out into every good work and God's calling for your life!

CONTACT JASON

For personal training, speaking events, testimonies, or faith and fitness seminars, contact Jason at www.workout2reachout.com

Works Cited

Alvidrez, Luis M., and Len Kravitz, PhD. "Hormonal Responses to Resistance Exercise Variables." *Unm.edu*. N.p., n.d. Web. 02 Feb. 2014. <http://www.unm.edu/~lkravitz/Articlepercent20folder/hormoneResUNM.html>.

Bernhardt, Gale. "The Real Reason You Should Warm Up." *Active.com*. N.p., n.d. Web. 14 June 2014. <http://www.active.com/triathlon/articles/the-real-reason-you-should-warm-up>.

Bryant, Cedric X., and Daniel J. Green. *ACE Personal Trainer Manual: The Ultimate Resource for Fitness Professionals*. 4th ed. San Diego, CA: American Council on Exercise, 2003. Print.

Colbert, Don. *Eat This and Live*. Lake Mary, FL: Siloam, 2009. Print

Hall, Susan J. *Basic Biomechanics*. 5th ed. St. Louis: Mosby Year Book, 1991. Print

Howley, Edward T., and B. Don. Franks. *Health Fitness Instructor's Handbook*. 3rd ed. Champaign, IL: Human Kinetics, 1997. Print

Kayla. "51 Fastest Fat Burners." *RISE & GRIND*. N.p., n.d. Web. 23 Jan. 2014. <http://eat-healthy-train-hard.tumblr.com/51fatburners>.

"Is Sugar Bad For A Bodybuilder?" *Bodybuilding.com*. N.p., n.d. Web. 13 Aug. 2014. <http://www.bodybuilding.com/fun/topicoftheweek69.htm>.

Munson, Jamie. "Why Gluttony Is a Sin." *Marshill.com*. N.p., 21 Sept. 2010. Web. 13 Aug. 2014. <http://marshill.com/2010/09/21/why-gluttony-is-a-sin>.

Olson, Jed. "Is Maltodextrin Bad for You? The Good, the Bad, & the Ugly - Fitness for Travel." *Fitness for Travel*. N.p., 07 June 2012. Web. 03 May 2014. <http://fitnessfortravel.com/is-maltodextrin-bad-for-you/>.

Powers, Tim. *Fit to Serve*. Seattle, Wash.; YWAM: n.p., 2009. Print.

Pruitt, B. E., Kathleen S. Crumpler, and Deborah Prothrow-Stith. *Prentice Hall Health: Skills for Wellness*. Glenview, IL: Prentice Hall, 2001. Print.

"Pullups For Total Beginners." *Scoobys Home Workouts*. N.p., n.d. Web. 10 Apr. 2014. <http://scoobysworkshop.com/pullups-for-total-beginners/>.

Quinn, Elizabeth. "What Is VO2 Max and Why Do Athletes Care?" *About.com Sports Medicine*. N.p., 16 May 2014. Web. 10 June 2014. <http://sportsmedicine.about.com/od/anatomyandphysiology/a/VO2_max.htm>.

Rosedale, Ron, MD. "Wise Up and Stop Eating Your Muscles for Fuel 7/7/05." *Mercola.com*. N.p., n.d. Web. 13 Aug. 2014. <http://articles.mercola.com/sites/articles/archive/2005/07/07/muscle-fuel.aspx>.

"Simple vs Complex Carbohydrates." / *Nutrition / Carbs*. N.p., n.d. Web. 13 Aug. 2014. <http://www.fitday.com/fitness-articles/nutrition/carbs/simple-vs-complex-carbohydrates.html>.

Taylor, Kimberly. "Gluttony: How to Be Set Free." *Take Back Your Temple Christian Weight Loss*. N.p., 06 Jan. 2009. Web. 13 Aug. 2014. <http://www.takebackyourtemple.com/how-to-be-set-free-from-gluttony/>.

The Holy Bible: Updated New American Standard Bible: Containing the Old Testament and the New Testament. Grand Rapids, MI: Zondervan Pub. House, 1999. Print

Vella, Chantal, PhD. "Exercise After-Burn: A Research Update." *IdeaFit.* N.p., n.d. Web. 13 Aug. 2014. <http://www.ideafit.com/fitness-library/exercise-after-burn-0>.

"Vitamins & Minerals." *Vitamins and Minerals: Understanding Their Role.* N.p., n.d. Web. 13 Aug. 2014. <http://www.helpguide.org/harvard/vitamins_and_minerals.htm>.

"VO2 and VO2max." *What Are VO2 and VO2max.* N.p., n.d. Web. 07 July 2014. <http://www.shapesense.com/fitness-exercise/articles/vo2-and-vo2max.aspx>.

Walker, Brad. "Proprioceptive Neuromuscular Facilitation." *PNF Stretching Explained.* N.p., n.d. Web. 27 Mar. 2014. <http://injuryfix.com/archives/pnf-stretching.php>.

Wilmore, Jack H., and David L. Costill. *Physiology of Sport and Exercise.* 4th ed. Champaign, IL: Human Kinetics, 1999. Print.

"What Muscles Do Pull Ups Work?" *PullupsZone.* N.p., 15 Feb. 2015. Web. 09 Mar. 2014. <http://pullupszone.com/what-muscles-do-pull-ups-work/>.

"What's the Difference Between Appetite and Hunger?" *Fitwatch.* N.p., n.d. Web. 13 Aug. 2014. <http://www.fitwatch.com/weight-loss/whats-the-difference-between-appetite-and-hunger-256.html>.